# THE ISLAND CROP DUSTING COMPANY
## DUSTING COMPANY
### EARLY AVIATION IN THE NORTH COUNTRY

## Jimmy Higgins

# THE ISLAND CROP DUSTING COMPANY
## EARLY AVIATION IN THE NORTH COUNTRY

Jimmy Higgins

# Copyright © 1996 by Jimmy Higgins

ISBN  0-7414-0341-2

*Published by:*

**INFINITY**
PUBLISHING.COM

*Infinity Publishing.com*
*519 West Lancaster Avenue*
*Haverford, PA 19041-1413*
*Info@buybooksontheweb.com*
*www.buybooksontheweb.com*
*Toll-free  (877) BUY BOOK*
*Local Phone (610) 520-2500*
*Fax  (610) 519-0261*

*Printed in the United States of America*
*Printed on Recycled Paper*
*Published  November, 2001*

On the frontispiece: Ernie Pretsch, the barnstormer and distinguished airline Captain, to whom this book is dedicated:

*He did the impossible.*
*He soared with eagles.*

\* TO PROTECT THE GUILTY SOME NAMES WERE CHANGED

# CONTENTS

# ILLUSTRATIONS

# INTRODUCTION

This is the true story of Ernie Pretsch, a young barnstormer, from Long Island, New York, who started an aerial crop dusting company in the potato country of Northern Maine in 1934 and a kid who just hung around and made himself useful.   While the airplane was fast becoming commonplace throughout the nation, in that neck of the woods and other remote areas, the airplane was still somewhat of a mystery.

The kid was born and raised in Caribou, Maine, a small village nestled in the flatlands of the Aroostook River Valley, spilling over along the valley's upper reaches.   Surrounded by beautiful green rolling hills, the valley was blessed with several lakes, within driving distance, and with more than ample forest land.   In the rich valley soil, farmers raised bumper crops of potatoes.

Ernie arrived in potato country during a time of great economic distress, not only in the local area, but throughout the nation.   This time of deep economic depression is also remembered as the "thirties."   Life was a daily struggle just to survive.   Thus, it had been hard for the kid to believe any of his dreams would ever bear fruit; yet, deep down inside, he never *really* lost hope that one day he would fly an airplane all by himself if he just worked hard and stuck to his dream.   But both Ernie's and the kid's dreams did come true, each in a different and unexpected way.

Ernie Pretsch, born in Germany, emigrated to New York in the twenties at the age of thirteen.   The desire to fly also burned deeply in his soul and it wasn't long before he found himself established as an "airport brat" at Roosevelt Field, the scene of many early historical flying events.   For the uninitiated, "airport brats" were a special breed of kids, who in the early history of flying in America, worked at a variety of jobs at airports; everything from running errands, sweeping hangar floors, baby sitting airplanes, washing and polishing, refueling, minor maintenance procedures and shoveling snow in the winter.   They worked for flight time only.   Bitten early by the flying bug, they all shared the common goal of learning to fly an airplane.   They toiled outside on flight lines despite cold winds of wintertime and hot sun of summer.

It made little difference to many of them that they wore the same clothing outside in the cold as they had worn in hot weather. Never complaining, always working from dawn 'til dark; ever waiting for the chance to fly.

# CHAPTER 1

## THE PREFLIGHT YEARS

For as long as he could remember, the kid had a longing to be busy, to be working at something or anything. One day, when he was twelve, after running some errands for Grandma Huston, she gave him a dime. On the way home, he stopped at a candy store to buy some goodies. A dime could buy lot's of candy. Inside the store, a farmer was talking with the store owner. He was complaining that he couldn't find anyone who could drive a team of horses. The kid chimed in: "I can drive a team!" Without batting an eye, the farmer said, "you're hired!" The kid was delighted. He had a job! He was somebody after all! He had driven a team on several occasions on his Uncle's farm.

The farmer drove the kid to his farm in an old green Reo truck. The kid hitched the team of big Belgian Roans to a large wagon and drove them down the hill to the field where the farmer was harvesting a big crop of potatoes.

Field hands loaded the barrels of potatoes onto the wagon and the long trip to the potato warehouses began. The team had to negotiate a long field road leading down to the highway. The unpaved road was rough and strewn with big rocks which had been dislodged by the spring run-off of melting snow. They were slowly descending a rather steep grade, when suddenly the right, front wheel became lodged against a big rock. The horses balked; they wouldn't budge. The kid jerked evenly on the reins and they began to move. Just as the wheels cleared the big rock, a Bee stung one of the horses on the rump.

The horses took off on a wild run down the rock-strewn field road, through a tunnel under the railroad tracks and out onto the highway. The kid jerked the reins, with his small hands, for a right turn and off they went in the new direction. The wagon skidded across the asphalt-paved highway until it hit the shoulder.

At that point, the wagon tilted up and nearly flipped over. All the potato barrels bounced off out into the field scattering contents all over the place. The horses never stopped. At long last, a little old man ran out onto the highway, at the outskirts of town, and held up his arms. The runaway horses came to a stop. How the kid managed stay on the wagon seat, through it all, was a miracle.

The kid turned the wagon around and drove back to where the load had spilled. Picking up all the potatoes that were visible or undamaged, he drove down to the warehouse located along the train yard. Slowly he inched the wagon on up to the loading platform.

A man came out to the loading dock from inside the warehouse. He lowered a foot and a half inch-wide wooden plank down onto the wagon. The plank now settled in at a steep 45 degree incline. The kid looked at the barrel then he looked at the plank and then on up to the man standing at the other end of the plank. The man said: "It's alright son, if you will grade the potatoes on the conveyor up here, I'll get the barrels up from the wagon." They worked it out.

For the kid, the long ride back was dreadful. How could he explain to the farmer what had happened to his load of potatoes? Arriving at the potato field, he had not gone far when the farmer came running down the field road screaming hysterically all manner of obscenities. Someone had apparently recognized the runaway horses and called the farmer with their version of the episode. The kid got the hint and took off, running to escape with his life. Thank God, the farmer never caught up with him. He would never have believed the kid's story about the Bee sting.

On another occasion, the kid just walked into a down town restaurant and began to work. He swept the floor, cleaned the counter and washed dishes until the owner ran him off, but as the kid reached the door, the owner called him back. "What did you think you were doing? the owner asked. The kid blurted out: "I just wanted to work!" Visibly puzzled, the owner answered: "But I can't afford to pay you!" The kid answered, somewhat stubbornly, "I don't want anything!"

Surprised, the owner said, "Well, if you want to work that badly, I'll teach you how to be a short order cook." The kid answered, "That's fine!" The kid worked on the restaurant counter until his first year in high school.

His short order cooking career came to an abrupt end one night. The high school baseball coach came in and said: "I can't have my ball players staying out all hours of the night. Go home and study hard so your grades stay above the eligibility level."

The kid asked, "Does this mean I've made the team?" The coach snapped back at the kid, "Yes, so act like it!" The kid's world turned around.  In the ensuing seasons, he became an outstanding athlete, gaining confidence with each passing day.

George Shaw, a World War I pilot, had become a local legend flying an early vintage airplane of the period out of a cow pasture just north of Caribou since about 1925.  He was the epitome of the flyer image Hollywood had projected on theater screens across the country.  He was tall, sported a thin, black mustache on his upper lip; was handsome and talented.  He wore the helmet and goggles, the white scarf about his neck, the boots and riding breeches.  To top it off, he claimed to be a World War I ace.

He flew a Curtiss JN-4, an open cockpit biplane, affectionately known as the Jenny.  The Jenny, built in 1916, was used to train World War I Army pilots. The airplane was a very stable but slow.  It was powered by a Curtiss OX-5 engine that pulled it along in level flight at a top speed of 75 mph;  not very fast by today's standards.  Thousands were built and could be had for $350 at the close of World War I.  The Jenny, never flown in combat, was very popular with barnstormers and was used to initiate the first airmail routes in America.

PHOTO:   AT THE OWLS HEAD TRANSPORTATION MUSEUM IN MAINE

Without a doubt, George was the father of aviation in the area. He was a leader in the eventual selection of the local airport site, the old cow pasture he had been using. In the mid-twenties and early thirties, George regaled town folk with all kinds of flying, performing many difficult aerial maneuvers that are relatively simple for today's airplane drivers.

For 25 bucks he would fly the more intrepid amongst the town folk, out over the town and back, and for an additional 10 dollars, he would throw in a loop and a stall. In the late twenties and throughout the thirties, very few of the locals had that kind of money.

George Shaw's tenure in the history of local aviation in the far north was still intact when the kid left home in 1939. Some of the stories that made him a legend were hard to believe; such as, the one that had him flying under the bridge, stretching over the river that flows through the town. Close inspection revealed that, because of the extensive structural configuration beneath the bridge, there was no room for an airplane. Yet, 'til this day, there are folks that swear they saw it happen.

George was, however, a hero and an inspiration to all kids in the area who wanted to fly. He was the area's first resident pilot and a great inspiration to those with a yearning to learn to fly. He was instrumental in the acquisition of land for development of the airport. He was also a gifted concert pianist who gave concerts for worthy causes.

Development proceeded and the pasture site subsequently became the first municipal airport in the state. The town had erected a big white clapboard hangar on the site. The building incorporated office spaces on each side at the front of the building. The structure was huge for that time and place.

The kid was an avid reader. Beginning at an early age, his mother nurtured his interests by acquiring a wide variety of books. In addition to books, he was deeply impressed by all the stories in the old pulp flying magazines. He bought them with money earned mowing lawns for the elderly in his neighborhood in the summer and shoveling snow off their sidewalks in the winter time.

Another source of exciting aviation yarns was a local character named Patrick Summers. Old Pat was a World War I veteran. He wore his old Army overcoat winter and summer and was always in need of a shave. Pat drove an old brown dray horse making deliveries of all kinds of merchandise.

Whenever the kid came across him, old Pat would spin some kind of a wild yarn about how he flew across the Atlantic ocean in a steam powered airplane returning home from the war in Europe. He said that, on the voyage home, they had to stop on a couple of Islands to chop down trees for fuel. Old Pat was way ahead of the science fiction crowd and the kid believed every word of it.

On his eighth birthday, May 20, 1927, his dad gave the kid a baseball, a bat and a fielder's glove. The kid was so excited he could hardly wait to try them out in a real ball game. After gulping down his breakfast, he ran to a nearby fence surrounding the Fair grounds at the end of the street. Half way up the fence, on his way to the baseball diamond, a man ran screaming from a nearby house screaming: "He made it! He made it!" The kid knew instinctively that Charles Lindbergh had landed in Paris on this the kid's own birthday. So now he had another hero to day dream about.

By the mid-thirties, many young barnstormers were arriving at the airport. Some were gone by sun up the next morning. And a few stayed on and became part of the activity connected with the airport; but in the end, they too were off to brighter horizons. They joined the stream of barnstormers who eventually brought flying to every nook and cranny across the country.

The airport was only a half mile from the kid's home. So every time the kid heard the far off drone of an airplane engine, he was on the spot as fast as his chubby little legs could propel his small body up the hill behind the house; arriving almost before the propeller stopped rotating, heart pounding with excitement, secretly hoping the encounter would result in earning an airplane ride.

After all, he reasoned, that when he greeted the circus in the railroad yard before daybreak every year, he had routinely gotten a job carrying big buckets of water to the elephants, in return for a grandstand ticket; even when he was so small he could barely carry a full bucket. But barnstormers were always on the downside of the next tank of fuel so it was hard for them to do any flying without a payload on board.

The biggest thrill of his life happened when a flyer, wearing a white scarf, helmet and goggles, with boots, riding breeches and a scuffed up leather jacket, would climb out of an old biplane with a parachute strapped to his back, and say: "Hey kid! 'Wanna' watch my ship while I go to town for some smokes?" Like an excited little pup, the kid would tremble all over. This, to his mind, was no ordinary human. This was God in all his glory.

Of course by the time the pilot "hoofed" it off to town, a crowd would gather. And people just had to find out what the airplane was made of, so they would poke at the fabric with fingers and tug on the propeller; they were in such awe of the machine. The kid had to caution them about cracking the painted surfaces, because on the older airplanes, some of the fabric was so thin you could spit through it.

Development of the airport at the old pasture site continued and it was believed that the town fathers had hoped that one day the airport would become the hub of a great transportation network in the sky. However, by the time the kid left to enter the Army Air Corps in 1939, that hope appeared to be remote. The runways were still grass, although runway boundaries had been clearly defined and marked. Air traffic was sparse. The airline had gone; many real and potential flyers were already serving in the military.

Shortly after World War II, the old wooden hangar burned down with tragic loss of life. An unmarried, pregnant weather observer was on the roof, taking readings from an array of weather instruments. The structure went up in flames almost instantaneously, like a bomb had exploded. There was absolutely no chance for her to escape. An investigation revealed that arson was the cause was the cause of the fire. The airport manager was subsequently convicted of the crime. He went to jail and served time for manslaughter.

During the World War II period, the east-west runway did get paved; could have been the result of some particular federal government project. In the end, a beautiful town, 12 miles to the south, became the jumping off base for Army Air Force flights over the North Atlantic to the war in Europe.

# CHAPTER 2

## THE OBSESSION TO FLY

Although the kid's only hero had been Babe Ruth, and he was already into sandlot baseball, his first up-close encounter with an airplane, had left him with an obsession to fly, by any means. By the time he had reached his tenth birthday Charles Lindbergh had joined the Babe as a hero.

The kid even built an airplane in the backyard, covered it with muslim fabric, used piano wire and pulleys for control of the rudder, elevator and ailerons. He carved a propeller from a short piece of, 2 x 4- inch, wood. He filched the little gasoline motor out of his Mum's Maytag washer. He discovered rather quickly though, that the motor lacked power to move the tiny airplane, much less fly it. So he decided on an "assisted launch" on the theory that, once airborne, the little motor would sustain the small "bird" in flight. The first snows of winter were not far away so he built a ski jump on the hill back of the house to serve as a launching pad. He put the tiny motor back in the washer and waited impatiently for the snows to come.

After what seemed a lifetime, snow finally arrived in the form of an enormous blizzard. His excitement knew no bounds. He would be the first ten year old in the neighborhood to fly his own airplane. In the dawn's early light, he reinstalled the little Maytag motor in the airplane.

And so it came to pass that, early on a snowy Saturday morning, the contraption, was moved up the hill back of the house. The kid remembered thinking, as he climbed aboard his little dream machine, that the excitement he was feeling must be something akin to what the Wright boys felt at Kitty Hawk, North Carolina, that cold, windy December day in 1903, as they made the final preparations just before their historical flight of 120 feet.

With everything now ready for the anticipated epoch-making flight, he started the little engine and nosed the airplane down the steep slope. As it gathered speed, he tested the controls. Nothing happened; that is, until it hit the improvised ski jump.

Suddenly, he was airborne. But in a flash, his unstrapped carcass was catapulted out of the wooden seat;

and continued in flight for several feet, like a big bird, into the side of the garage. Since it was only the top of his head that made contact, there was no physical damage. His body spent more time in flight than the airplane. So intent was he on achieving flight his planning had not taken into account how the contraption was going to clear, if airborne, all the obstacles in the line of flight.

Dismayed, but undaunted by the disaster, the determination to become airborne, one way or another, still burned within. And then another bright idea was birthed in his spirit: parachuting. He could float off the rooftop of the house and land on the front lawn. It might not be as exciting as flying an airplane, but nonetheless, it would be flight of a sort and less dangerous to life, limb and to the property. So using fabric, salvaged from the failed airplane project, he fashioned what he believed to be a proper parachute.

He climbed to the top of his little Sears and Roebuck-built house and rolled the make-shift parachute into a round bundle. Two short lengths of rope were stretched between his body and the fabric, where he was to hang beneath the great canopy he had fashioned, while floating gently back to good old terra firma as though on a soft white cloud.

In a split second, without thought, which was to sort of become the trademark of his life, he tucked the bundle under his arm, wrapped the ropes around each of his wrists, and quickly plunged over the side of the roof. Contrary to expectations, he plummeted straight down, like a one-ton bucket of lead, whereupon, he sunk up to his knee caps in his mother's flower garden with the bundle of fabric still under his arm. Right then and there, he vowed to never again to take up parachuting, as a hobby, a profession or for anything else.

Being the unofficial greeter at the airport kept the kid busy. Important folks were beginning to fly in with more and more interesting airplanes. Barnstormers he met were asking him to do more for them, but still, that longed for airplane ride, appeared to be remote. But hope remained strong as ever. And although he didn't know it, at the time, that part of his dream was just around the corner.

# CHAPTER 3

## THE CHICAGO TRIBUNE TRI-MOTOR

The kid's first ride in an airplane came about by a strange twist of fate. When he was 12, in 1932, Colonel McCormick, owner and publisher of the Chicago Tribune newspaper, flew in for some fishing on the Allagash, a wilderness river about 80 miles northwest of the local airport, as the crow flies. The river was a magnet for "sports" from all over the country. Flying the Colonel's airplane was Jimmy Collins, a Naval Reserve pilot. The kid was on the spot before the airplane rolled to a stop in front of the hangar.

They were an awkward looking pair, as they stepped down out of the big, blue tri-motor, with the Tribune's logo splashed over the fuselage. The Colonel looked like an over-stuffed Teddy Bear, in his late fifties. He had gray hair and a round face adorned by a well-trimmed cookie-duster mustache. By contrast, Collins was tall, rather slender, and perhaps in his late twenties. He had sharp, intense blue eyes that seemed to see right through you. Collins later became a test pilot for Grumman Aircraft at Bethpage, Long Island, New York.

A Maine guide met them at the airport. He wasted no time hustling them into a station wagon and quickly leaving for the long ride up north to the river where they traveled to the Allagash by canoe. The Colonel and Collins spent two weeks on the river. When they returned from their fishing trip, they quickly loaded their equipment and their bounty of fish into the tri-motor and prepared to get underway. But when Collins cranked up the right outboard engine, there was a blast, like a loud backfire. Black smoke poured out of the engine and the propeller stopped rotating.

The Guide was still there waiting for the big bird to take off. There was a hurried conference in the hangar office with Collins, the Colonel and the Guide. When they emerged, the Colonel was whisked away by the Guide to the train station for the long trip home to Chicago with his box of fish in the baggage car, packed with dry ice. Jimmy Collins remained on the scene to monitor repairs to the airplane.

A middle aged machinist, was sent up from Long Island, New York. As a retired Navy Chief, who owned an aircraft engine repair shop, he was also a consultant to the Navy on aircraft propulsion systems. The Chief arrived at the airport with some of the necessary parts for repair and installation in the damaged tri-motor engine. The problem turned out to be the failure of an internal engine component. Some additional parts had to be sent up from New York.

Watching the Chief work was like seeing a great surgeon practicing his skills in an amphitheater. He repaired the engine before an ever growing audience and stayed on until after the run-in time was completed and throughout the flight test. Jimmy Collins was on the scene early every morning. He never spoke to anyone except the machinist working on the engine. With summer waning and with the engine finally repaired, Collins started it up.

Following completion of the required run-up time, the moment had arrived for the flight test. Collins looked around at the watching audience. Looking right at the kid with those sharp blue eyes of his, and with a big grin, he selected some of the kids for "ballast."

The kid was first, one of the lucky few. Lucky? He had been at the scene from daylight until dark daily since the big airplane had arrived. He strapped himself into one of the wicker seats laced with plush padding. He was so excited his body was shaking all over like a little puppy about to get his first cookie.

It was the kid's first ever airplane ride. As they circled low out over the town, he was thrilled right out of his little mind, in spite of being labeled only as "ballast." The kid was never been able to explain the sensation he felt upon leaving the ground, for the first time, in an airplane.

Jimmy Collins died out over Long Island just before World War II. He was testing an airplane for the Grumman Aircraft Company. Jimmy was a great guy who liked kids. The kid will never forget him or his first airplane ride.

The summer of 1933, saw a major increase in air traffic at the airport. All the new traffic pushed the kid's desire to fly an airplane to a new heights and he was more determined than ever to get up there somehow.

One air show featured an Autogiro, one of the first off the production line. The Autogiro had made only a slight impression on the public who treated it as some kind of freak. Also a Gee Bee racing airplane came in, sponsored by the Shell Oil Company. At the time a rumor circulated around town that the Gee Bee was piloted by Jimmy Doolittle.

One of the most impressive airplanes to arrive was a Grumman Navy Helldiver flown by Boyd Pierson a local Naval Reserve pilot. He came in from the Squantum Naval Air Station in Massachusetts.

An aerobatic team of a father and his cute little 15 year old daughter, put on an impressive show. The young blonde girl was also an accomplished wing walker thrilling large crowds that gathered from all over the county and parts of New Brunswick. With the increased airport traffic, the desire to fly an airplane burned even deeper into the kid's mind.

A couple of Ford tri-motors also paid a visit to the airport that summer. The Ford tri-motor was also known by local comedians as the "Tin Goose." One tri-motor featured a Maytag appliance sales promotion and flew over the area dumping several thousand handbills out the door. If a lucky person recovered a handbill with a ticket of some sort attached, they could win a new washing machine. The kid never heard of anyone finding the magic ticket.

The other tri-motor had the name "The Smiling Through" emblazoned on its fuselage. It was used to fly passengers out over the area on sight-seeing tours. Many airplanes of the era were named by their owners much the same as boats are today. One such airplane, a Fokker tri-motor called the Southern Cross, flew nonstop from San Francisco, California to Australia in the thirties.

One of the visiting tri-motor pilots was the famous aviator, Clarence Chamberlin. He and another pilot had made an unsuccessful attempt to fly the Atlantic to Europe, however, Chamberlin later made a successful flight flying a Fokker tri-motor.

The first big event of the summer in 1934 was ushered in by the arrival of a Royal Canadian Air Force (RCAF) squadron of DeHaviland Tiger Moth training airplanes. They were driven down by a cold front which suddenly materialized in their flight path. They landed one by one, and quickly lined up along the fence in front of the hangar.

No sooner had crews installed the tiedown kits when all hell broke loose. The wind was fierce. They watched and worried from inside the hangar as the small airplanes strained at the tiedown ropes. Golf-ball sized hail, accompanied by thunder and lightning, poured down from the sky. In a matter of minutes all the fabric was completely stripped from the small biplane trainers. It appeared as though the airplanes had been ravaged by flame instead of wind and hail; otherwise, no apparent structural damage was visible.

A couple of days later, RCAF vehicles arrived with ground crew mechanics. They returned the pilots back to their home base, somewhere in New Brunswick, Canada. The crews spent nearly all summer restoring the airplanes to flight status. The kid learned a lot about airplanes from the maintenance crews: ran errands and hung out with them as they went about their jobs and he learned to rib stitch fabric to airplane wings. When the repairs were approved and the airplanes returned to flight-ready status, the RCAF vehicles again arrived, this time to deliver the pilots and haul the mechanics back to home base.

Early one evening in 1934, near the end of summer, the kid was home reading a pulp magazine called "Flying Aces." A tremendous roaring noise abruptly jolted him back to reality. He immediately assumed the noise was being made by several airplanes circling the area, although no airplane, heard in the past, had never been that loud. The kid jumped from the chair and pitched headlong out into the darkness but was unable to determine what was really going on. He did a quick run up over the hill to the airport. A large crowd had already collected and was growing larger by the minute. Overhead, fire from the exhaust stacks of several airplanes, big ones, could be seen.

Duke Solomon, the pudgy Fire Chief, had already arrived with the rest of the volunteer fire department. Duke quickly sized up the situation and determined that the runway needed some lights on it. Several cars, filled with the curious, were commandeered and dispatched down the runway where volunteer firemen lined them up opposite each other across the runway. The headlights provided the runway with enough light for the airplanes to safely land.

And in they came, one after another, until thirteen Army Air Corps Keystone bombers, from Mitchell Field, Long Island, New York, had successfully touched down. They quickly taxied up the small hill at the end of the runway to park up against the fence in front of the hangar.

The Keystone bomber was an ungainly behemoth: a biplane with two outboard Liberty engines. The engines were equipped with short exhaust stacks which explained the horrendous noise when they flew over the house. The Liberty was a huge liquid-cooled power plant, each generating 420 hp.

The big bomber was built by the Keystone Aircraft Corporation. It carried a crew of five; a gunner, bombardier and a wireless operator with two pilots, positioned side by side, in an open cockpit, out in front of the wings. It was huge, very slow (114 mph top air speed) and difficult to maneuver. The Keystone formed the backbone of the US Army Air Corps Heavy Offensive Command in the "thirties." According to Jane's Encyclopedia of Aviation, some of them were still on active duty in the Philippines when World War II began.

The bomber squadron out of Mitchell Field had encountered unexpected head winds during the flight and thus had arrived later than estimated. Weather forecasting was still in its infancy; at best, a hit and miss proposition.

The Squadron Commander said they were circling the field until someone got the bright idea that the Fire Chief came up with, otherwise God only knows what their fate would have been. They were quite rapidly running out of fuel. So much for Army cross country flying in 1934.

The next summer would see an unexpected development at the airport which changed a lot of area lives forever. A flyer was coming who, with his dynamic personality and great flying skills, would inspire a great many youngsters to seek careers in aviation and some to make great wartime contributions to aviation.

# CHAPTER 4

## THE ISLAND CROP DUSTING COMPANY

Early on a warm day in June 1935, the kid climbed the hill back of the house heading up to the small pasture that was now the village airport. School had just let out for the summer and was hoping that somehow he could get some kind of a job, with or without pay, working around airplanes. Summer had exploded upon the valley. The big elms along the streets, provided a cool canopy of green. The birds were back and everywhere the wild flowers were once again in full bloom.

During the severe winter of 1934-35, when the winds howled all night long, blowing snow up over the windows of kid's little house he dreamt of flying off to some warm tropical paradise. Little did he know that one day very soon he would be doing that very thing in Central and South America. Typhoid and the other diseases like diphtheria, measles, mumps, chicken pox, scarlet fever, and pneumonia all took their toll among the kids and the elderly. At home the kid's family was quarantined when the kid's and his brothers came down with measles, mumps and scarlet fever; but at different times, stretching the confinement period nearly to the end of winter. In the Spring, losses among classmates were always counted as students toiled to make up for lost time.

The kid's poor dad! He was forced to spend most of the winter with Grandma Huston. Although sometimes he would come to the family after dark. They would talk; shouting at each other across the street. He would leave things for them at the edge of the lawn and hurry away lest he get trapped into the quarantine. In fact, quarantine was where the family spent Christmas that year.

But summer came at long last, though each year winter always seemed longer and more severe than the year before. Although the kid had no hint of what was about to happen, this summer would see his life changed forever.

A lone barnstormer flying a DeHaviland Gipsy Moth had arrived the day before, and he was hurrying to see if the pilot had something for him to do. As he crested the hill, the kid's ears picked up the steady, far-off drone of an airplane engine somewhere south of the valley. His sharp blue eyes scanned the skies, over the southern horizon, at the entrance to the river valley. Soon, he could see a small speck in the distance.

His heart began to pound with excitement. He completely forgot about the Gipsy Moth pilot and his airplane. Hurrying to the corner of the hangar, overlooking the runway, he arrived just in time to see an open cockpit biplane, with orange wings and black fuselage, "grease in" to a landing and roll out to the end of the field.

The airplane taxied back down the runway and on up to the front of the hangar. The kid watched with growing excitement as the pilot climbed out of the cockpit and removed his parachute. His heart was pounding so hard it hurt; his throat was so dry, his tongue stuck to the roof of his mouth.

There was something about this guy that was different from all the others that he had seen. He had the helmet, the goggles, the white scarf, the leather jacket; but the boots and riding breeches; where were they?

This guy was wearing khaki slacks and blue tennis shoes with white soles. But there was another thing, besides his blonde hair and all-American good looks, that set this guy apart from the others who had come and gone. He had a suitcase. To the kid, it was a sign that the pilot had come to stay, at least for awhile.

The kid stood there, mouth agape, blue eyes watching and wondering. Suddenly, the pilot turned and looked right at him. With a great big, toothy grin, he said: "Hi kid! Do you live around here?" The kid gulped. "Yep!" he replied, "all my life."

Without another word, the pilot turned back to his airplane and began to push it into the hangar. The kid ran to help him. And somehow, right then and there, the kid knew that the pilot and he would become great friends. He felt like a great cloud with a silver lining had just floated his way.

Next day the kid was at the hangar bright and early. He walked over to the big black bird with the orange wings. She was dirty but beautiful. He learned from the placard on the instrument panel that this airplane was a Curtiss Travelaire with a 300 hp Wright J6-7 engine.

Rummaging around, inside the hangar, he found some rags that belonged to some unknown barnstormer. He cleaned and polished the big airplane (now his baby) until she sparkled in the early morning sun. Just as he was putting the finishing touches on the job, the new guy rode up in a car with someone.

Approaching the kid with a puzzled expression on his face, with a sweeping motion of his arm over the airplane, he asked, "Did you do this?" The kid nodded affirmatively. "Well I'll be damned!" the pilot exclaimed, reaching into his pocket, as though fishing for a coin. Seeing this, the kid protested: "No! No! I don't want anything." The pilot asked, "Then why did you do it?" Without blinking an eye, the kid replied: "Because I like airplanes."

The newcomer commented: "Well you certainly do good work!" Then he said something that, to the kid's ears, was like beautiful music: "How'd you like to help me today?" The kid nodded affirmatively. Then, the pilot said, "My name is Ernie, Ernie Pretsch. What's yours?" "Jimmy!" answered the kid.

Throughout the day they worked together on the airplane getting it ready for the conversion into a crop duster. Besides being an expert pilot, the kid learned that the new guy, Ernie, was an excellent carpenter. And together, they had built a plywood hopper that was to be positioned in the front cockpit of the Travelaire.

Toward the end of the day, Ernie paused from the task at hand. Looking over at the kid, he asked: "Well Jimmy, how'd you like to learn to fly?" The kid was delirious: "My Gawd!" he sighed. "Great! wonderful!" or words to that effect, the kid stammered. "Good!" Ernie said, "just stick around, make yourself useful and I'll teach you how to fly."

Later that day, as they walked down the hill towards town, Ernie explained his vision for the future of the company he was going to build: "I'm going to operate the airport. Initially, we'll be dusting crops this summer. Some other guys are on the way. Soon we'll be in the charter business, doing some bush flying and we'll be teaching people to fly airplanes. Perhaps next year we will be the regional sales representative for Piper Aircraft. How's that?" The kid was speechless.

In the days that followed, the plywood hopper was inserted into the front cockpit of the Travelaire, thereby converting it into a crop duster. Ernie also designed and perfected the venturi device that would suck the dust out of the hopper and distribute it evenly over the crops.

Ernie impressed the kid as being one very smart guy. The kid noticed that while Ernie had little patience with stupidity, of which the kid certainly qualified, he was quick to forgive and forget. He had sharp, piercing blue eyes and a blonde mop of hair. Nothing much got past him.

If he said it once, he said it 100 times: "Kid, if you make a mistake while working on an airplane, don't try to cover it up. Someone could get hurt or be killed. Speak up as soon as it happens. No one will ever punish you for telling the truth." The kid also learned that Ernie was 24 years old and that he had a wife named Mary who was a school teacher in Long Island, New York. Born in Germany, he had migrated to America as a child. When it came to flying an airplane, Ernie was one of the most intense person in the world. He remained focused until the bird was back in the barn.

The next arrival that summer was mechanic, Edward A. Clarke from New York. Red was the color of his hair and so it was his nickname. He was a big, gentle giant, over six foot tall with a burly build, like the proverbial fullback. Red was the first mechanic to work for the Island Crop Dusting Company.

The kid became Red's helper. He was a master aircraft and engine mechanic. Red taught the kid a lot about airplanes and what makes them fly. Under Red's close supervision, the kid kept busy working on inspections, repairs and performing preflights on airplanes. Red was a great teacher. He talked the kid through every maintenance procedure while it was being performed.

Shortly after the dusting season ended that first year, Red Clarke left for greener pastures. He later became Chief of Maintenance for a major division of Northwest-Orient airlines. Before he left, Red gave the kid a classic shotgun which he treasured. Unfortunately it disappeared after he left for military duty in World War II.

Seth Yerrington came in soon thereafter. Seth was Ernie's business partner. He flew a few crop dusting missions but was mostly a charter pilot. He was a real suave guy, sported a thin black mustache that made him appear like a "hot shot type" pilot to a lot of people, but Seth was nothing of the kind. He was a good pilot and an immaculate dresser; always looked sharp.

It was rumored that, in the early days of prohibition, like many other unemployed flyers, Seth flew illicit cargo from Canada into the United States. He was eventually caught, fined and had his pilot's license suspended for a time. Seth was especially good to the kid. He never talked down to "the kid," as he was called by everyone, and let him fly whatever airplane they were in at the time, every time he could.

Seth was sort of aloof. Never hung around the office with the rest of the guys at the end of the day or on the rainy days when they were confined to the office area for the never ending stories about flying, mostly barnstorming and crop dusting yarns.

During World War II, Seth worked as a flight instructor at Spartan School of Aeronautics, under contract to the military services. He was a good story teller and an excellent pilot. Last the kid heard, Seth had retired and moved to Florida.

That summer Matty Springer came up from New York; Matty's baby face and small stature made him especially attractive to the girls. They all wanted to mother him. Matty was built like a horse jockey, with dark eyes and black hair. Despite the fact that Matty was very short, he had amazing strength. He could wrestle the 50 pound sacks of crop dust into the hoppers with the best of them. He always flew with cushions to move him up to the controls, especially to the rudder pedals. He was a good pilot, working towards a commercial license.

Matty and the kid became great friends, working, fishing, hunting, and double dating whenever time from their busy work schedule permitted. They worked together as a team throughout that summer and on through the winter. They worked at whatever Ernie told them needed to be done.

Matty was from a place in New York where a worm is called a "woim." His father was President of one of New York's boroughs. Mr. Springer came north one time for a short vacation. Matty and the kid took him out fishing a couple of times. He always wore a business suit even to go fishing. They always got a chuckle when Mr. Springer called out to Matty: "Pass the woims, Matty!"

Clarence Sproul arrived from New Jersey that spring, He was flying a Stinson Detroiter. The Detroiter was a high wing monoplane powered by a 200 hp Wright Whirlwind engine. He and Ernie converted the four-place Detroiter into a crop duster by removing the rear seat and installing a plywood hopper and venturi device.

Sproul was tall, had dark curly hair and, and according to the local female flock, was quite handsome. He appeared to be a loner; very professional and much too sophisticated for the Island Crop Dusting Company gang. He did his job every day and when it was finished, took off for places unknown. Someone said that Sproul had gone to Princeton University. In any case, Sproul certainly had the "ivy league" ego and all of its persona which, stated in a nutshell, loudly proclaimed, "superiority."

Other pilots arrived for the crop dusting season including: Eddy Glini who came in from somewhere in New Jersey. Ed was a scholarly, brooding gentleman with a dark complexion. He detested time wasting. He left after that first season of flying "dusters".

Ed Glini became a Corporate pilot for IBM after World War II. Ed always got after the kid about wasting flight time. He advised him to do something worth while with his flying time; always shouting at the kid: "Practice! Practice! Practice!" each time he saw the kid heading out to fly. The kid listened and learned.

Ed died in an accident some time in the sixties while taking off from the airport in Anchorage, Alaska. He was flying a Lockheed Hudson at the time. It happened just after he had dropped off some IBM executives who were going big game hunting in the area.

"Slim" Burns (not his real name) arrived, following the crops north. There was no mystery about why his nickname was "Slim." He was tall and skinny with blue sparkling eyes; looked like a farmer from out of the hill country of North Carolina. Slim had a marvelous sense of humor.

He used to barnstorm out in the Dakotas, where, according to him, a big, heavy logging chain was tied to the wind sock. When the chain was horizontal and whipping around in the wind, he said they'd quit flying for the day. Slim Burns was a walking treasure of barnstorming lore. He knew all the barnstormers, from Charlie Lindbergh to the current crop in the mid-thirties. What great stories he told.

Skip Henderson (not his real name) arrived from Georgia, also following the crops north. Skip was a tall, good looking guy, with sand colored hair, graying at the temples. He appeared to have an unquenchable thirst for southern style corn "likker." Frequently, Skip would get a small crate from Georgia via Railway Express. The crate was always marked: "AIRCRAFT COMPASS! HANDLE WITH CARE!" Actually, the crate contained a gallon can of corn liquor which was really 90-proof alcohol; powerful stuff. Skip never drank on the job or on the day before he had to fly "dusters."

Besides sharing the "likker" with some of the gang, in the evening, Skip loved to play practical jokes. A classic example of his sense of humor, as a practical jokester, was the one he played on a small, dapper older gentleman. The old timer would walk over to the newly acquired Stinson Reliant, as the crew watched through the shop window.

With a furtive look over his shoulder to see if anyone was watching, he opened the airplane door and took a quick look inside. Then, very cautiously, he would close the door and hurry from the scene. This ritual was carried out every noon for more than a week.

Early one morning Skip went out to the Stinson. He removed the rod that ran through the piano-type hinge that attached the door to the door post, then, he carefully pushed the door back in place. Noontime came and the crew gathered at the shop window. In due time the little old guy arrived. He went through his routine. But when he opened the door, which was very light, it came off the airplane.

He stood there, as though frozen, with the door in his hand, and an expression of shocked surprise on his face; then, sheer terror hit him. It was awful. Hands trembling, he pushed the door back in place and fled the hangar like his tail was on fire. They never saw the old gentleman again. The kid found the whole episode funny but, at the same time, a little sad.

Lee Munsey came in from Brooklyn, that summer. He was flying a snow- white Curtiss Challenger Robin which was one of the most reliable airplanes of the period. Munsey had a freckled face and sand-colored hair. He was a fun-loving, practical joker, almost funny enough to be Irish.

Lee was an excellent pilot who dusted crops throughout the summer. When it came to flying, Lee had his serious side. The crew and Lee hit it off right from the start. Several times, the kid loaded dust during Lee's dusting operations and then moved back to watch him fly over the adjoining fields of potato crops. He always did a fine job.

The Challenger Robin was the airplane that Douglas "Wrongway" Corrigan flew across the Atlantic to Ireland in the 1930s. "Wrong Way" was how the press dubbed him when he told them he had really intended to fly to California from New York, but got mixed up and flew in the opposite direction.

Slim, Skip, Lee and Ed  followed the crops from south to north and back again:  beginning in Florida with tomatoes,

22

they followed the growing seasons up the Atlantic Seaboard to Georgia and South Carolina with cotton; tobacco in Virginia and North Caroline. They then moved up to Long Island, New York and on up into Maine for the potato crops, something like the migrant apple pickers of old. The pilots were great at the kind of flying they did, given the equipment with which they had to work.

One day when the whole gang was hanging around the office the kid decided to go out flying. But once outside, he noticed that the wind sock was straight out so instead he returned to hang around the office to soak up the folklore that always came out on those rare occasions when all the gang got together.

When the kid came back, Slim asked, "Why ain't you out flying?" "Too windy!" replied the kid. "Shucks! out in Nebraska we used to hang a logging chain on the wind sock. When the chain was horizontal we'd quit flying." "I thought that was done in the Dakotas," the kid retorted. "Might have been," retorted Slim.

With all the actors on stage, the curtain was about to go up on the first activity of its kind. Airplanes would be in the air over the valley almost constantly. The airport would never be the same again. Summer air traffic would increase enormously in the next several years, until after World War II and a few years beyond.

# CHAPTER 5

## DUSTING CROPS IN NORTHERN MAINE

The following year, during the summer of 1936, the organization grew into a real company. They were growing at an exciting rate going into the second year. The missions now covered not only crop dusting, but flight instructions, charter flying, barnstorming, bush flying, aircraft repair and maintenance, airline servicing operations and Piper Cub sales and service.

Ernie had picked up more airplanes; a J2 Cub with a 40 hp continental engine, a Stinson six-place passenger/freighter powered by a 425 hp Pratt and Whitney Wasp engine, 2 Curtiss Robins powered by 180 hp Challenger engines, a Stinson Reliant powered by a 300 hp Wright J6 Whirlwind engine. It had a beautiful glossy black fuselage and a black wing color scheme with a bright yellow trim. The Reliant was a semi-gull wing model. The company also acquired a blue Model S, Waco cabin biplane on floats powered by a 225 hp Wright Whirlwind engine. The Waco was still flying in Alaska in 1989.

The Island Crop Dusting Company was still under contract with a huge potato company to apply dust to about 8000 acres of potatoes. That company in turn was under contract to provide potatoes to The Atlantic and Pacific company who provided their bounty to all the Atlantic & Pacific stores across the country.

The Island Crop Dusting Company had become extremely busy in a hurry early in the summer. Again, Matty Springer and the kid traveled with the pilots to the fields where the dust was to be applied, usually in the early morning or late evening when wind conditions were calm.

They worked every day from before dawn, until the morning breeze came up, and again in the evening until dusk, except when it was raining or windy. By the time they arrived in early morning to dust crops, the farm crew would have copper sulfate dust loaded on trucks in 50 pound bags. Matty and the kid loaded the dust into the airplane hopper and then jumped down to the ground to swing the propeller for the pilot.

All summer, they traveled to the local fields with the car, a 1932 Model A Ford. It was rough, dirty work that turned sweat into a light green coating on the skin. The coating wouldn't come off. It had to wear off. Crop dusting was really catching on in the area.

When the dusting jobs were outside the immediate vicinity, Matty and the kid flew out with pilots to help load dust and swing the propeller to start the engine after they emptied each load out. They rode out "piggy back" on the pilot's shoulders in cramped cockpits. That summer Ernie's slogan was: "You load it! I'll fly it!" The kid loved every minute of what he was doing despite the sweat and dust.

In early summer, on one such trip, with the kid riding on Sproul's shoulders in the Stinson Detroiter, they flew out to a farm, just east of the Canadian border, to dust a potato crop. On the way back home, Sproul suddenly peeled off and landed in a tiny hay field at the edge of the vast forest that covers northwestern Maine. Adjacent to the field, was a small farm house made of logs, along side a shed or small barn. Obviously, someone was establishing a farm there. When the airplane stopped rolling, Sproul said to the kid, "Get out and wait here! I'm going south for the night! I'll have someone pick you up." Sproul had just met a girl and couldn't wait until evening-time to be with her. He was probably having a hormone fit.

In somewhat of snit, the kid watched the Detroiter roll across the hay field climb out and bank low heading to south. Of course, the kid thought, it would only have taken him an extra 15 minutes to fly back to the airport. But that was Clarence. And as Jimmy Durante, the old comedian, used to say: "when ya gotta go, ya gotta go!"

The kid stood in the small field from about ten O'Clock in the morning until late afternoon, and all the while, a bright hot sun passed overhead. During all that time, a young Frenchman, his wife, with a small boy, presumably their kid, stood quietly and motionless, staring at him.

They had come out of the house when the airplane arrived. Apparently, they spoke no English and for certain, the kid spoke no French. He felt strangely uncomfortable under their gaze. Perhaps they were ready to defend their property, with their lives, from the ravages of some alien invasion from the sky.

French Canadians in that neck of the woods had never before seen an airplane or its contents up close. At any rate, the kid was greatly relieved when, just before the sun disappeared over the horizon, Ernie arrived with the Cub to fly him home.

In the "good old days," airplanes flown by the Island Crop Dusting crew were not equipped with electric starters. Engines were started by swinging the propellers by hand. Only a couple of the Island Crop Dusting Company's airplanes were equipped with the inertia starter. They were the non-crop dusting types.

The inertia-type starter was operated by a hand crank which translated its energy to the engine by use of a clutch arrangement operated by the pilot in the cockpit much the same as the electric starter, except for the application of arm power. Electric starters were added to later production aircraft.

Sometime in the thirties, aircraft engine starting was made easier by the installation of a device called a booster. This device was used to send an extra charge of current (a spark) to the top cylinders just as the propeller blade was being pulled through by someone swinging it.

Some boosters were initiated by turning a small handcrank while other were operated by pressing a button-type switch. On Sproul's Stinson, the booster was initiated by the pilot punching a button on the instrument panel. Timing was critical. The guy in the cockpit had to use caution that the charge was initiated at the right moment else the man swinging the propeller could be severely injured.

One hot, sweat-soaking day, Sproul was flying dust out of the airport to a nearby farm. He came in for a load of dust. The kid loaded the dust into the hopper and jumped down to swing the prop for him. The engine was red hot. As the kid placed his hands in position on the propeller, suddenly, without warning, the engine backfired. He could have sworn that Sproul hit the booster button prematurely which would account for propeller kick-back. But then the kid was prejudiced.

Sproul and the kid were constantly at war though, silent as it was, none-the-less it was real from the word GO. He saw the kid as a big nuisance. The kid saw himself as a hard working kid who was helping to make the company a success so he could be there forever. So they could never agree on anything.

At any rate, the kid couldn't get his hand off the blade soon enough, and as a result, was knocked down. When he got up his little finger was lying across the back of his right hand which was covered with grease and copper sulfate dust. To make matters worse, Sproul wrapped a wad of dirty, grease-soaked waste around the kid's hand.

Sproul's only remark was: "They shouldn't let these damn kids hang around here." They rushed the kid to the hospital where a fight began to save his hand because infection was already established. They shot massive dosages of antibiotics into his backside. Some of the cute little student nurses felt so bad about it they cried while they were attacking him with needles.

A few days later, the doctors began the long, tedious operation to re-attach the finger to his hand. The doctor had said that he was not sure the operation would be a success. Later, when the kid woke up, he couldn't feel his hand. All he could see was the end of a splint board wrapped with bandages. Self pity immediately over-whelmed him and the kid began to cry. "I will never be able to pitch baseball again," he bawled.

A crusty old nurse sitting by the bed asked: "What are you bawling about? There's a little boy in the next room whose legs were cut off at the knees this morning by his father's mower. You don't hear him whining do you?" The kid turned off the tears in shock over the vision of that little boy going through life without legs. As far as the kid knew then, he had only lost his little finger.

At that point, the doctor came into the room. He pulled up a chair and said: "The operation was a success but you won't be able to use the little finger again. In fact it will be frozen stiff in a down position, at a 90 degree angle. In a few weeks, we'll be able to remove the board. You can go home tomorrow."

Eventually, through a lot of work, over several months, by exercising the bent digit, breaking down the adhesions, the kid was able to get it almost into the normal straight position. It remained crooked and stiff but never got in the way of anything. In fact it helped his curve ball.

That summer The Island Crop Dusting Company somehow acquired a rooster and he quickly became the mascot. The rooster was a beautiful big Rhode Island Red with bright, shining red feathers with a green tinge about the neck. He would strut around the apron in front of the hangar where he would become airborne in the prop wash of airplanes being run up during pre-flight test.

Someone bought a bag of corn kernels from the local feed store so he could eat regular meals, like the rest of us. They called the rooster "Big Red." He would sometimes close in to the rear of a particular airplane being run up on the ramp, spread his big wings, and become airborne, sometimes performing a loop just to show off. At times he landed on his back, but more often he wound up on his feet.

Skip shared his "corn likker" with "Big Red," the rooster, and perhaps it was inevitable that someone would soak the kernels of corn with the "likker" and feed it to "Big Red." Under the influence, "Big Red" stumbled around, staggering like the proverbial drunken sailor.

"Big Red" eventually died of acute alcoholism on a day especially made for him: a Barred Rock hen had shown up, ready for action. But "Big Red" wasn't interested. All he wanted was a couple more kernels of corn soaked in Skip's "corn likker." Someone obliged with more alcohol soaked kernels and "Big Red," seeing the Barred Rock hen, made one mighty effort to crow, but flopped over on his back with his feet stuck straight up in the air, and he was gone to that great roost in the sky.

Not even the beautiful hen could revive him. "Big Red" had died. Must have been sclerosis of the liver. Before sun down the next day the Island Crop Dusting Company crew were in the hangar eating roast chicken. No doubt the "cannibals" had cooked him with a welding torch.

Whether it was a barn in mid-field or big elm trees surrounding a potato patch, Ernie could weave a pattern of copper-sulfate over a field like a spider spins a web. At times it seemed that the wheels were parting the plants.

A news reel camera crew set up a platform one time in the middle of a potato field from which they were going to film a crop duster in action. They installed the camera and equipment on the platform and signaled for action. Ernie flew so low they jumped off the platform and fled the field in terror.

You can travel around the country and overseas, watch professional crop dusting pilots, some flying the modern Grumman AG dusting machines, none will ever match the flawless performance of Pretsch, the crop duster, back in the thirties. Ernie modified his own airplane and it did the job, smooth as silk. Some folks said he should have been born a bird.

More action was developing at the airport. And little did they know, that they were about to enter into modern day air travel. Caribou airport, it was reported, had become the northern most airport in the "forty-eight" states and the northern most Port of Entry for air travel.

# CHAPTER 6

## THE BOSTON & MAINE AIRLINE

In 1937, Boston and Maine (B & M) Railroad, decided to try the airline game. B & M began airmail and passenger service to northern Maine from Boston, Massachusetts. They came in with Stinson "T" tri-motors sporting yellow wings with black fuselages. Actually they flew into central Vermont and billed themselves as Boston and Maine, Central Vermont Airways. But as far as this story goes, it's B & M Airlines.

The airplane, later designated by the manufacturer as the Stinson Airliner, was powered by three 260 hp Lycoming radial engines. It could haul eight passengers and a single pilot. And it's a safe bet that it couldn't cruise even a tad above 100 mph. Today there are airliners that travel faster on the ground.

The Island Crop Dusting Company was awarded the airline's servicing contract. Initially, the kid and Matty filled wing tanks by hand, pumping it up from 50 gallon drums of aviation fuel flown up from Boston in the airliner's baggage compartment.

PHOTO COURTESY E.C. SMITH

30

Later, B & M installed an electric pumping system and ground tankered the fuel in. Sometimes, the kid also did the pre-flight engine warm up and "mag" checks before the pilot came on board. In spring and winter, the old Stinson-T airliners were equipped with tire chains.

With the new fuel pumping system, came directions to daily pump out five gallons of gasoline to remove condensation from the tank and pipe lines. The kid and Matty then strained the five gallons through a chamois cloth to remove any moisture and used it to fuel the J2 Cub for their own flying time.

Before the airline came in, however, the Station Manager, Arthur Herman, arrived and soon became busier than a hound dog overwhelmed by fleas. He established a modest weather forecasting station. Radio communication with Boston was established and Art was in business. He became the B & M Airline dispatcher, weather forecaster, and station manager providing the weather reports to Boston, handling the baggage, selling tickets and assisting the loading and unloading of mail and passengers.

Caribou was the turnaround terminal for the northern leg of the airline's route. There was a two hour layover before departure to the south. Airline passengers would sometimes arrive quite early for the flight south. The airport was the only exciting place for miles around.

On one such occasion, the kid was out in the hangar sitting in an old Eagle Rock airplane fuselage located against the back hangar wall. When Ernie began to teach the kid to fly, he suggested that the kid just sit in the airplane and play with the controls; to get the feel of them so that manipulating the airplane controls in flight would become second nature, so to speak.

So the kid chose the old Eagle Rock out in the hangar. No one seemed to know who owned the old relic. The airplane had a big Hispano Suiza, liquid cooled engine, that could generate 400 hp. Several times he had heard flyers talking about building a racing plane around that engine. But like so many aviators of that era, who had those kinds of dreams, they were never converted to actual ideas and action.

But there were a few flyers then who had dreams, that when converted to ideas and action, built airlines, designed new aircraft that stunned the world, and converted big dreams into aircraft factories and new aerospace industries that still dominates global aviation and space programs to this day.

The old "hangar queen" still had the engine, landing gear and wheels, black fuselage, seat, stick, throttle and rudder controls intact, missing only the wings. The kid was out hangar-flying the "Hangar Queen" one day when an older,

32

stately looking gentleman, awaiting the next airline flight out, spotted him. He walked over to where the kid, with his fertile imagination, was flying high above the clouds.

With a smile he said, "Son, you're flying too low!" The kid told him what he was doing and went on to describe in detail, despite his lack of knowledge, all about the theory of flight, with some fanciful embroidery thrown in. The gentleman listened patiently and graciously as the kid rambled on, describing how the rudder worked, how the elevators worked and how to make an airplane turn, dive and climb. Why, this man appeared to be eager to learn all about airplanes, and the kid was really educating him.

He was asking questions from time to time as further proof to the kid of his lack of knowledge about airplanes and how to fly them. As he turned to leave, he thanked the kid for answering his questions and for the interesting information he had provided. Only later did the kid learn from the airline dispatcher, that his visitor had been the great aviator, General Olds, who later commanded a flight of big bombers around the world.

One note of interest concerning the old Eagle Rock: one day four guys from New Jersey arrived at the airport with a bill of sale for the old bird. They spent two months reassembling the old relic and working on the engine. They flight tested it for an hour and then took off for New Jersey with three guys on board.

A few months after they left, the Island Crop Dusting Company received a postcard telling us that they had arrived home after surviving 32 forced landings along the way.

Captain Don Stewart, was the first B & M Airline pilot to come in. Captain Stewart was a big guy, very friendly, and very well educated;  liked to play golf with George Shaw during the two-hour layover in Caribou.

Hazen Bean was the second Captain to come in flying the tri-motor airliner. He quickly became known as "Beanie" to the Island Crop Dusting Company Crew. Beanie was an all around friendly guy. He was an asset to the airline because he was always selling air travel.  His real, outgoing personality worked magic with the passengers.

PHOTO COURTESY E.C. SMITH

Beanie spent the two-hour turnaround time hanging out with the Island Crop Dusting crew. He was a great source of information for the kid, always giving him advice about what to do with his life.

He was an Air Corps reserve pilot and naturally wanted the kid to enlist in the Army Air Corps, because whether or not Roosevelt knew it, Beanie saw the draft and war coming. He counseled the kid to enlist to go to Panama for two reasons: 1). The kid could return to his baseball career in two years, barring war, and 2). He could get training in aircraft mechanics. The kid enlisted as Beanie had advised.

A few years later, World War II was on. Beanie had become a Major in the Army Air Force. He and the kid met in Houston, Texas one night, in 1942, during the war. The kid was on the way home from Panama on an emergency leave. One leg of the journey, terminated in Houston. He was in the airport coffee shop nursing a cup of coffee, killing time, before the over night flight out to Boston. Suddenly, someone slapped the kid on the back. Startled, he turned to see who it was and there stood "Beanie" grinning from ear to ear. He was in uniform, with US Army Air Corps insignia, and on his shoulders were the gold leafs of a Major. He told the kid that he was ferrying a Douglas A-20A airplane from California to LaGuardia airport in New Jersey for the Army Air Corps.

They had quite a reunion. It was the only time the kid ever encountered an alumnus of The Island Crop Dusting Company/B & M Airline circle. It was an exciting encounter that he will forget. The crowd in the coffee shop must have thought them drunk.

However, getting back to the story. In the year of the kid's sixteenth birthday, Dorothy Parker and Sinclair Lewis, both famous writers of the "twenties" and "thirties," flew in on B & M airlines to spend Christmas at his cottage in Rimouski, Canada on the St. Lawrence river.

Mrs. Parker was queen of the one line "zingers" as wisecracks were called in those times. She was a writer with a real toxic tongue; a member of the Broadway literary cadre in New York city, the self-anointed literary center of North America, if not the entire planet. Sinclair Lewis was a famous writer and also a member of the same literary circle of noted authors with whom Mrs. Parker traveled. When the airliner carrying the celebrated authors arrived at the airport and taxied up to the unloading area, Art Herman, the airline station manager, was ready with the portable step that passengers used to step down onto out of the airplane in those days.

Pulling the door open as always, Art stepped back to greet the passengers. Everything was proceeding as usual until Mrs. Parker, arms filled with packages, stepped down on the portable step. At that moment, her skirt suddenly began to slide down. In fact it dropped down around her ankles. She had unbuttoned her skirt in flight so as to be more comfortable and had apparently forgotten to button it up again.

Art was momentarily stunned. Then he reacted in a panic. He removed his uniform tunic and attempted to wrap it around her hips. She responded, yelling out in a loud voice:

"Young man, take your hands off me!"   There she was, standing with her skirt around her ankles. Her arms were still loaded with packages;  one of Art's arms was about her hips and the other across her fanny.

Mrs. Parker, of course, was trying to be funny but Art was extremely shy.   He finally held her bundles while she adjusted the skirt to its proper position. We dared not kid him about it afterward.   In due time, Ernie flew the happy couple up to Rimouski, Canada along the Saint Lawrence river in the Curtiss Robin which was equipped with skis.

After Christmas, Ernie once again flew up to Rimouski to pick up the famous couple and bring them back to the airport. They boarded the airliner immediately. As soon as they were seated, the kid started the engines and began the preflight routine, warming up the engines, checking the instruments, and performing magneto checks.

Dorothy Parker, observing the situation in the pilot's compartment, exclaimed, loudly: "My Gawd!  That kid isn't going to fly this thing to Boston is he?" Stirred up quite a commotion. Some of the other passengers looked anxiously toward the exit.   Captain Hazen Bean, however, showed up in the nick of time. When Mrs. Parker saw "Beanie," she calmed down and decided to remain on board as did the other passengers.

The kid shut the engines down and gave up the seat to Captain Bean.  As the kid walked back down the aisle to leave the airplane, he couldn't help but give Mrs. Parker his best look of disgust.   Her reaction? She smiled and winked. He smiled back.  She, no doubt promptly forgot the incident, but the kid will always remember that day with Art and the other incident in the pilot's compartment.

Shortly after the incident with Mrs. Parker, Art left the airline and was replaced by E. C. Smith.   E.C. was quickly dubbed "Smitty" by the Island Crop Dusting Company Crew. He soon established a first rate weather station at the field and quickly assumed all the other duties.   Once Smitty gave the kid a crash course in basic fundamental meteorology so he could substitute for him in an emergency or if he should take a vacation.  He never took a vacation nor was he ever sick so the kid missed the opportunity to be an airline dispatcher with all the side duties that the position entailed.

Smitty was a positive influence on the kid's life. After the B & M airline eliminated the northern-most stop, Smitty went to work for the airline in Boston but later on, he moved over to the CAA as an Air Controller at Logan Airport in Boston.

The US Weather Service took over Smitty's weather station and used it without modification for several years. Smitty was valuable to any aviation oriented business.

Crop dusting was beginning to slow down. The Potato Company developed financial problems and the contract was in limbo. Charter flying and student training was now the mainstay of the company. Some of the leased equipment went back, and the future looked bleak but some dusting work remained.

# CHAPTER 7

## LEARNING TO DRIVE A CAR-THE HARD WAY

Early one morning, when the kid had been left behind to watch the hangar, he got a phone call from Ernie. He yelled: "We've had an accident! We're 10 miles on Route 1 out towards Presque Isle. Put the spare Robin propeller in the rumble seat of the Buick and bring it out. Look for us on the right in a field near the highway. Get here fast! It's urgent!" The kid answered, "But I don't know how to drive." Ernie screamed, "LEARN!"

The Buick was a 1933 model convertible with a stick shift. Now, the kid could fly an airplane but didn't know how to drive the more complicated automobile. There was no one else available and Ernie had said to get there fast.

The kid ran out and struggled with the propeller and finally wrestled it into the rumble seat as instructed. He jumped into the roadster. After some fiddling around, he finally figured out how to start it. He pushed the clutch pedal in and stepped on the starter. With engine running, he let the clutch out. The car hit the hangar. He moved the stick and tried it again. Same results. At that point, Smitty came bellowing out of the airline office yelling: "What the hell you trying to do?"

Banging the hangar with the car had probably upset some of his sensitive instrumentation. The kid gave him Ernie's message.

"Get out of the car! I'll show you what to do!" Smitty commanded. Smitty, was really shy. The kid had never heard him raise his voice, much less, to cuss. He quietly did his job thoroughly with a great deal of dedication to his profession and with no nonsense. Smitty backed the car away from the hangar and talked the kid through his every move. He then headed the car toward the highway and got out. The kid slipped into the driver's seat and moved out onto the highway.

Getting to the destination seemed like forever, and luckily, he met very few cars. He hardly dared move his eyes from the road ahead. But, when he did, the car almost left the road, a maneuver that apparently had attracted the attention of a State Highway Trooper, who had nothing else to do.

The kid was only vaguely aware that someone was behind him such was the terror of his first attempt at driving an automobile; his eyes were locked onto the road ahead. The trooper had followed him to his destination, but strangely, never pulled the kid over. His hands were frozen in a death grip on the steering wheel. At last, he saw the airplane up ahead and steered off the road into the field adjacent to it. He jumped out of the car and hustled back to the rumble seat.

To his surprise, the highway trooper was already at the back bumper waiting for him. His greeting was: "I've been following you for the past eight miles and it appears you don't know how to drive a car. I'd like to see your driver's license," he added. The kid answered, "I don't have one." "I thought so," the trooper retorted.

Before the trooper could say anything else, Ernie came bounding across the field, and yelled, "Grab the end of that propeller officer, we've got an emergency over here." It seemed someone had nosed the Robin over while taxiing across the rough sod in the field next to the potato field.

The kid relaxed. However, his freedom was short-lived. After watching them install the propeller, the Trooper turned back to the kid. "You know you need a license to drive a vehicle on the highway don't you?" said the Trooper. "No! I don't need one. This is the only time I have ever driven a car and it will be the last. This was an emergency and no one else was around to drive the propeller over here," the kid answered. The trooper looked as if he had swallowed something that didn't get all the way down. Finally, he said, "I'm not going to arrest you this time. But don't ever let me catch you driving again without a license!"

Delivering the propeller to Presque Isle in the old Buick roadster, however, was just the beginning. The kid was sent to town several times without benefit of a license or any driving instructions.

But one day while returning to the hangar from a trip to the hardware store, the same Trooper followed him right into the hangar. "I'd like to see your license," he said. "I don't have one," the kid answered. "Listen kid!" he said, utterly exasperated, "Either you've got to get a license or I've got to give up my job, and I love my job." The kid shuffled his feet around, deeply embarrassed, and mumbled: "I would get a license officer, but I don't have any money."

Just then Ernie came out of the shop. When he saw the Trooper, Ernie asked, with all the innocence of a small child, "What's he done this time, Lew?"

Lew Howard had an open, friendly face with sharp blue eyes that were now blazing with frustration. "He is still running errands for you guys and still driving without a license," answered Lew. "As a matter of fact," he said, "why don't you guys give him the two bucks and I'll take him to the DMV for his license and then we can stop all this nonsense right now."

Ernie reached into his pocket and pulled out two crumpled dollar bills and handed them to Lew. Probably the money for his next meal.

Lew drove the kid to the Department of Motor Vehicles, about 10 miles away, in the police car. As they walked up to the window, a clerk looked up and asked: "Can I help you?" Lew handed the clerk two bucks and said: "Give this kid a driver's license!" The clerk gulped and asked the kid a few questions, typed some words on a form, and handed him the license. No driving test was required.

On the way back to the airport, the kid asked: "Lew, now that I've got my license, how about letting me drive?" Lew took a audible deep breath and said, "You know, I've a good mind to stop this car, pull you out and kick your backside all the way down the road. I may do it anyway when we get back if you don't smarten up."

Lew became one of Ernie's flight students and he and the kid soon became fast friends. Lew even took him out on patrol with him sometimes. He could always spot a guy driving without a license, sometimes at long distances: He would say, "They just don't look natural." He also said that if he couldn't talk to the culprit first to try and get him to change his attitude about driving without a license, he would turn in his badge. The kid realized then that he had been a real test for him, and because of Lew, he permanently changed his attitude.

Lew Howard died during WW II over Germany flying a B-24. An odd twist to his story is, earlier, when he was on a flight to Africa via Brazil, an accident that wiped out the entire crew with the exception of Lew. Over Germany, when his airplane was shot down, only Lew failed to make it out. He will always be missed until the day the last of those who knew him have passed on.

Meanwhile, in between jobs, running errands and baby sitting lame airplanes the kid, was getting flying lessons from Ernie. Progress was slow because Ernie was busy juggling three business problems at the same time and the kid, working with Matty, was also busy. But they were making progress and the bottom line was close at hand.

# CHAPTER 8

## LEARNING TO FLY

During the summer, whenever he had a few minutes between dusting jobs, and problems, Ernie and the kid took the Piper Cub out for a flying lesson. The kid loved that little yellow J2 Cub. It had become a part of him. Right from the first, on this session, Ernie gave the stick and throttle to the kid and said, "Take me for a ride!"

After a few more short lessons, mostly touch and go, landings and takeoffs, the great day finally came. It happened long about the time of his 16th birthday. He and Ernie were out shooting landings and takeoffs. After, what the kid thought was a poor performance, the Cub rolled out to a stop. Ernie got out of the airplane and simply said, to the kid's complete astonishment, "Go do it! You're on your own!"

The kid taxied back to the end of the runway, turned into the wind and pushed the throttle wide open. After a short run, he eased the Cub off the ground. As he circled the airport, he thought: "My Gawd! It's pitiful how little I know about what I'm doing." But he went through the motions as if Ernie were still sitting behind him looking over his shoulder; a feeling that stuck with him throughout his flying career. By the time the kid landed, he was so excited he couldn't recall exactly what it was he did even a few minutes afterwards. All he knew was he had just achieved the object of his obsession: to fly an airplane all by himself.

Ernie was still standing where he had been left. The Cub rolled up to where he was standing. As he climbed aboard, he yelled: "Congratulation, kid!" They taxied back to the hangar where the guys were waiting to initiate the kid into their circle, although he realized he never could begin to match their levels of skills and experience.

For the kid there was no experience on earth like soloing an airplane for the first time. The feeling of exuberance and the wave after tidal wave of freedom that swept over his soul. It was the greatest experience on earth sort of like the day he had fallen in love for the first time. The dream the kid had doubted could ever come true had indeed materialized.

The gang got him a little drunk on some of Skip's corn "likker" all the way from Georgia. They took him home to ease the way with his mother because of the corn likker. It turned out that she was more upset with the kid being up in an airplane by himself, than she was with the incidence of booze, even though neither of his parents would ever allow booze in the house. She forbid him to fly again but his Father told him, with an aside, "It's all right son, you keep right on with your flying. I'll work it out with your mother."

His dad, as a railroad engineer, sat behind the throttle of big steam locomotives hauling high speed express trains and big freights, which was about as close to flying, without leaving the ground, as you could get. So he understood the kid's desire to fly. His dad taught him lessons that directed him to the higher ground in all matters of life. To the kid, flying was real and complete freedom. In those early days there was no air traffic to worry about. They were free as the birds, landing in open fields anywhere and everywhere.

After much study and flying practice, a few months later the kid was ready for his license test. The big day arrived and he completed the written test. Some of the pilots had advised him to bypass the Private pilot's license, to go for the Limited Commercial ticket. The CAA Flight Examiner gave him a very high score on the written and oral test. After the oral part was passed, they went out for the flight test.

The flight Examiner talked the kid through a series of maneuvers designed to test his flying skills; vertical turns, stalls recovery, spins, and above all else, to keep his head moving on the alert watching for other aircraft.

When the Examiner chopped the throttle to simulate engine failure, the kid responded by setting up an approach to a suitable nearby field. The flight examiner praised his reaction to the simulated emergency, gave him a thumbs up salute and directed him to return to the airport.

They arrived at the hangar and the kid followed him into the office. The examiner closed the door and told him to sit down. He said: "You demonstrated excellent flying skills, very good knowledge of regulations and related information, however, they say you need some time to mature. With this advice in mind, I am going to deny you the Limited Commercial license and instead issue a Private Pilot's ticket. In 6 months, when I return here, I will issue the other license. You won't have to take any further tests. Also, for your information, the Limited Commercial is going to be eliminated and converted to a Commercial license next year."

However, before the six months was up, the kid was in the Army Air Corps in Panama earning $20.75 a month. He lacked a half hour flying time for renewal of the Private Pilot's license so the license was taken away. A month later, the flight time renewal requirements for pilot's serving in the military were eliminated. The draft had begun and now military service was patriotic. Prior to the draft military service was considered to be for bums looking for someone to feed them.

Intrepid big brother Wendell was the kid's first passenger which, beyond a shadow of a doubt, proved that neither of them had all their marbles in the right place. The kid's dad, had always expressed a desire to see the great forests of northern Maine from aloft, so he became the kid's second passenger. His dad had missed his first calling; working in the woods. He and the kid's uncles had worked for the Great Northern Paper Company as Cruisers in years gone by. They went into the woods for weeks on end marking older trees in a particular area for harvest.

The kid's father died shortly after he took him out flying. His was a long illness with great suffering. In fact, it seemed, that the kid had never known him when he was completely well. In those days there were no sick benefits. If one missed work, he didn't get paid. His dad always remembered that flight. He was especially impressed with the vastness of the timber stretching unbroken as far, in all directions, as the eye could see. He could not believe the sight he saw from the small airplane at 3500 feet altitude.

As time passed by, there were adventures in the wild blue to be pursued and the kid pressed it to the fullest possible with the Cub and whatever else was available at the time. The kid meant to test his newly acquired wings with cross country flights. A lot of wistful little guys the kid saw staring longingly at an airplane got rides. He also flew all the snooty little girls in his high school class who had always snubbed him at school. They just happened to be sightseeing at the airport. Of all the kids that he took out flying, several made careers in aviation.

One little guy was "Abe" Daniels who later distinguished himself as a Marine Sergeant pilot. Abe became a highly decorated hero in the Pacific, during War II. While flying an obsolete Douglas Scout Bomber on a dive bombing mission in the battle for the Solomon Islands, with only a rear gunner on board, he came upon a flotilla of Japanese Destroyers. Flying straight in, he laid three bombs on the mid-section of one of the Destroyers. It burst into flame went down to the ocean floor.

A few weeks later on another mission in the area, he was forced to ditch in the ocean when the engine failed. He was badly injured when his face contacted the bomb sight which was located a few inches from his face.

He and his gunner were in a rubber raft for a indeterminate length of time and eventually made landfall where they were helped by a tribe of natives on one of the outer Islands in the Solomon group. A few days later, Abe gathered some white rocks and arranged them on the beach to read "DAN" his nickname.

He hoped that by some strange miracle a squadron buddy would fly over and see the rocks. He was lucky. The rocks were seen from aloft and the word was relayed to a PT boat cruising the area. Abe and his gunner were rescued.

After some time was spent in the hospital, recovering from injuries, he was returned to flying status. Abe was awarded the Distinguished flying cross and the Gold Star, in lieu of a second Air Medal. Abe was recommended for the Navy Cross but the recommendation was never processed. Perhaps the Navy caste system took over at some point during the process.

He was subsequently promoted to First Lieutenant and returned to the States where he was eventually assigned to combat school in California as an instructor. There, he was again promoted and transferred to take charge of an Aerial Gunnery school in El Centro, California. He served a successful mission there. By war's end, Abe had climbed the ranks to Lt. Colonel as commandant of an aerial gunnery training facility. Not bad for a kid from the small village of Caribou, Maine who learned to fly with Ernie Pretsch.

# CHAPTER 9

## FLYING ADVENTURES AND MISADVENTURES

On a beautiful, clear day in late summer, a day built for flying, the kid rolled the Cub out of the hangar and headed north for a few miles to get away from the growing air traffic at the airport. He had been practicing vertical turns, loops, rolls and simulated forced landings near the airport in the past, much to the irritation of airline Captains, and a few others.

PHOTO COURTESY E.C. SMITH

The kid became so engrossed in what he was doing that he failed to keep a watchful eye on the weather which could radically change without warning in that part of the world.   Suddenly, without warning, he encountered severe turbulence that nearly flipped the Cub over on its back.  After recovering to a more stable flight attitude, he did a "180" and his heart leaped into his throat.  All around him were black boiling clouds, huge thunderheads.   And now the little airplane was being tossed about like a chip on a turbulent sea.

Looking for a safe spot on which to put down, he saw a small field almost beneath the airplane.  From a cursory glance it appeared rectangular in shape and was nestled underneath the crest of a 30 degree slope, out on the leeward side of a large hill.  Without further thought, he chopped the throttle and made a dive for it.

As the Cub floated in over the trees, he slipped it down hard, flaring out onto the turf.  The little airplane had no brakes but the tail drag did its job.  The up-hill roll stopped inches from the trees at the end of the field.  He picked up the tail of the Cub and pulled it as far into the woods as possible for protection from the coming storm.  As it turned out, the good Lord was still watching over fools.  The airplane was sheltered from the wind and just a few big drops of rain fell. He had landed diagonally up the slope; providing the longest possible takeoff run.

The storm quickly passed over.   Faced with the dilemma of how to get out of a postage stamp sized field, he had to make up his mind on one of two courses of action: whether to walk several miles to a phone and call Ernie to come get him out or come up with a way to get out on his own.

While pondering the problem, he checked out the situation, just as Ernie had taught him.   The field was relatively dry and he saw nothing that would slow the Cub down on the take-off run.  So he walked the takeoff route looking for rocks and other obstacles.  He noticed something about the trees at the lower corner of the field, and slightly to the left. The tree tops seemed to melt away on one side.

There appeared to be traces of an old tote road, choked with young saplings.  He figured right away that when he did get it off the ground, he might be too close to some of the bigger trees to get up over them.  So, he decided that banking to the left, along the old tote road, was the best way out.

For the moment, the wind had died down and the air seemed heavy.  In fact, it was perfectly still.  Not a single leaf on the trees surrounding the field so much as rustled. He walked back to the Cub. Turning, he took one more look down the slope to confirm what he had just surveyed. Pulling the Cub out of the woods, he turned it around facing diagonally down the slope, hopefully, his only path to the wild blue and home.

Standing against the wing strut and behind the propeller, he reached up and gave it a swing. The little engine purred like a kitten. He let it idle for awhile to really get the engine warm, then climbed into the front seat and buckled up. Pushing the throttle wide open he simultaneously moved the stick ahead. The little Cub responded instantly and it was rolling down the slope with the tail high. As the big trees seemingly loomed up overhead, the kid hauled the small bird off the ground. Again the Cub responded and became airborne, but the kid's problems were still out there. Too late he realized that the Cub was not going to gain altitude fast enough to clear the trees. Instinctively he slapped the stick to the left and booted left rudder; then backed off a little on the rudder pedal until the Cub was nearly vertical when it slipped out through the saplings on the left side of the old tote road.

Tree tops were scraping the wing bottoms, as the Cub broke out over an old abandoned gravel pit, where it caught an updraft of air. The little bird went up like a kite flying in a stiff breeze. The kid turned south and high-tailed it back, dodging thunder storms, to the safety of the hangar; like a small baby bird going home to the safety of the nest and its mother. He wiped beads of sweat off his brow.

The kid flew several other airplanes which included a Curtiss Junior, a pusher-type airplane, powered with a little 45 hp Szekely engine. The Junior was owned by a young local kid. The little engine was mounted on a small airfoil-designed tripod attached to the wing center-section near the trailing edge. It was a two-place open cockpit bird with very slow forward speed, and at times when the wind was right, it could move backward at a very good clip.

The Curtiss Junior was an ugly looking airplane with long dirty aluminum colored parasol-type wing with a faded black fuselage. It looked as if it had missed several of the required inspections which by law had to be performed by licensed aircraft mechanics.

The owner didn't have a license to fly but he hauled little folk like the kid around in it all the time. He also rode a mean looking motorcycle, wore a black leather jacket, white scarf, boots and riding breeches.

Although the owner could fly, he wasn't particularly good at it. The kid didn't realize the guy's ineptitude until he was given a ride in the Junior; however, they were forced down when one of the engine mount struts buckled. Luckily, they were close enough to the field to float safely on in onto the runway.

The Curtiss Junior was actually a power glider so with the proper skills it could remain airborne without the help of the engine for several miles under the right thermal conditions. The kid was miles out from the airport once when one of the little tripod struts, on which the engine was mounted, broke at 2500 feet altitude. He chopped the engine and floated back in over home field with no stretch at all.

One time the kid took a little "cherub" for a ride. Because of the pusher-type airplane that it was, the little guy was given specific instructions not to leave his seat until he was helped out of it. Otherwise, he might walk into the propeller.

But the cherub became so excited, that before the bird stopped rolling, after they returned, he jumped out. The kid had cut the engine switch. But unfortunately, the propeller kicked back one more time and smacked the little cherube beside the head as he ran past it. The kid heard the propeller hit the little guy. Sounded like a baseball bat connecting with a watermelon.

The kid reached out for the cherub's little body to keep him from falling. But he ran right on past him. The kid tried to catch him but the cherube out-ran him, and the kid could really move fast in those days. Yelling only made him run faster. For days the crew watched but neither his parents nor the little boy ever appeared. They had thought sure the little guy was badly hurt.

The kid sort of became the owner's pilot for a short time. Anytime the owner wanted to go someplace, he would have the kid take him in the Junior. So it came as no surprise that one day he wanted to go to Boston to take the Private pilot's exam. On the day he chose for the trip, the wind was extremely strong and the kid advised against flying. But the guy insisted on carrying out his scheme to get a license. So the kid agreed to fly him there. It wasn't clear that he had even made an appointment to take the test from the FAA Examiner.

They took off without incident and climbed out of the pattern very slowly, against ever increasing wind pressure. They steered south for a few miles and "zap" like running into a brick wall, they stopped in mid-flight, hovering, like a big bird about to drop onto the nest. The head winds were too great for the little "puppy" with the big wings.

The kid pushed the throttle full open but they were still drifting backward. When they drifted back over the end of the north-south runway, the kid nosed the airplane down into a sharp dive with the throttle to the firewall. Slowly, they inched back over the fence at the end of the runway, but the Junior would not settle down onto the turf. A couple of the guys watching the dilemma from the hangar, ran down to where they were and literally pulled them down onto the runway. They laid over the fuselage as the kid taxied back to the hangar.

Ernie was extremely angry. He ended his lecture with the tidbit that the owner was nearly broke and had expected the kid to pay his own expenses. The kid shuddered at the thought because he too was broke. Being broke and stranded in Boston would have been a disaster.

The kid flew the Curtiss Junior a little bit more that summer. One good thing about the "little bird" was its buoyancy. If the engine quit, which it often did; from 2000 feet, it could literally glide back to the airport from anywhere in the County. Despite the good gliding characteristic, the little Szekely engine, mounted at the trailing edge of the wing, was in a fragile position; like skating on thin ice every day, waiting to break through.

The struts on the airplane wing would buckle every few hours or so because of the extreme vibration from the engine. When this happened the pitch of the engine sound would change. At the exact moment the sound pitch changed, the pilot had to chop the engine switch real quick else the prop would chew up the trailing edge of the wing and other nearby parts. So flying the Junior kept the pilot on his toes.

On another day, a small drama was about to unfold around the great novice pilot the kid had become. Early on a Sunday morning, as he walked toward the hangar area, he heard a couple of guys arguing. The argument was about the flight characteristics, or lack thereof, concerning a shabby looking old Curtiss OX-5 Travelaire biplane. The old biplane had arrived a few days earlier, in mid-summer 1937, piloted by a young Canadian barnstormer named Norman Farnum. After barnstorming around the country, the old bird had come to roost in the pasture, also known as the local Municipal airport.

Farnum was a young very friendly, outgoing guy and very shortly became "Norm" to the crew. He was the very proud owner of the airplane in question that morning. On the ground he was a rollicking, completely undisciplined kid. He had just come in from another town where he had partied all night, drinking home made brew. Norm and a fellow Canadian, Fred Flake, who was a perennial student at The Island Crop Dusting Company, were having an intense discussion about the flight characteristics of Norm's OX-5 Travelaire, and how easy it was to fly the thing.

Freddie Flake, who can only be described in the most charitable way, as the most magnificent jerk the kid had ever known. He will always be remembered for his many facets of low human behavior. But in that time and place, he was way ahead of himself. In today's society of deceit and double speak, he would be a  perfect fit.

Freddie can only be described as a small minded man, filled with envy and jealousy. He possessed the forked tongue of a snake.  He could spin a poisoned yarn about somebody he didn't like that could ripple outward, washing over his victim in its wake. Like all cowards, he loved to utterly destroy people with his tongue.  Rumor had it that the reason he loitered so long over his flight training, with his father paying for his upkeep and training, was perhaps a way to keep him out of the Canadian draft.  He was always a shadowy figure sneaking around the place.

Fred apparently had made some snide remarks about something concerning Norm's airplane that the kid didn't quite hear. The next thing he heard was from Norm, who saw him coming;  "Why that kid over there (pointing towards the kid) could easily fly this airplane, even without check ride." Said Fred, the snake, a little more heatedly,  "Bet he can't!" "How much?" asked Norm. "Betcha five bucks!" said Fred. "You're on!" answered Norm.

Next thing the kid knew they were strapping a chute on him, and over the rim of the cockpit he slid, dropping down into the bucket seat.  Norm swung the prop and the tired old OX-5 wheezed alive. The engine could put out 90 hp if it was in good condition and could pull the airplane along at about 75 mph maximum air speed. After a lengthy warm-up, during which the kid prayed every prayer in his Sunday School repertoire, he taxied out to the east-west runway and kicked the rudder to turn the old crate around into the west wind.  After another magneto check, he slammed the throttle full open.

The truculent old bird soared heaven-ward like a half-hearted, sick turkey running into a slow breeze.  "My Gawd," the kid said to himself, "I've never even had a ride in this thing, much less, been checked out in it.  As a matter of fact, the only thing I know about this beast is that it has only two throttle positions: *wide open* and *closed*."

With the throttle wide open, the old biplane could make an optimistic 90 miles per hour.  The real truth was, the kid had 15 whole hours solo in the tiny Piper Cub.  The kid didn't realize, until he was racing down the runway that, here were two guys who may have been betting his life away: Fred, the ass,  was betting he would get killed, drunken Norm was betting that he would make it.  But like Ernie always said, "Flying's like riding a bicycle. If you can ride one you can ride em all."

The flight around the field that Sunday morning was a long one.  But the kid  greased the old bird in, "hot pilot" style.  That landing was a complete accident, mainly because immediately afterward, he could not remember ever really seeing the ground.  He taxied up to the hangar just in time to see Ernie charging around the corner of the hangar like a mad bull.  He parked the airplane, slipped out of the chute, climbed down from the cockpit, and went off to face Ernie.

Ernie yelled at Norm, then Freddie Flake and the kid: "If you guys ever do anything like this again, I'll kick all your butts all the way down the hill."   Norm collected his five dollar bet and off he went down the hill without the benefit of Ernie's boot.

Flying different airplanes without a checkout, while still a novice at the flying game, was a stupid thing to do in every sense of the word: airplanes, like women, have hidden, unique characteristics that make them dangerous unless you know what to expect.

The kid always expected a surprise while flying both civilian and Army airplanes; saved his neck a few times.  Maybe that's an instinct that develops naturally while one is learning to fly.   Despite Ernie's threat, the kid occasionally flew the Travelaire.

A month later, while flying Norm's OX-5, The kid was forced to land on Highway, Route 1 because of rapidly developing adverse weather conditions and nowhere else to go. As the kid dropped down on the approach, he could see ahead that no cars were approaching. He flared out above the road and killed the engine, just in case the airplane veered off the road and nosed over.

Ahead, on the left, was a gas station;  the old fashion kind, with the big over-hang, that extended out to the edge of the road.  As the old bird "zipped" silently past the building, the kid saw a guy sitting in a chair tilted back against the building.  When the old Travelaire rolled out past him, he was so surprised that he and the chair slid down the wall onto the ground, and he was lying flat on his back.  Shortly thereafter, the tail skid dropped down onto the asphalt, spraying sparks out the rear like a giant roman candle.

The airplane had no brakes and continued to roll, gradually slowing to a point where it could no longer be steered with the rudder pedals. The high crown configuration of the road made it impossible to control the airplane.

Highways up north were so designed to flow water from the melting snow of springtime into the deep ditches along the roadside.  Eventually, the ship slid off the road and came to rest against a patch of tall, green corn.

The filling station man helped move the plane back to the leeward side of the building where it rode out the storm. Later, he walked down the road to hold traffic so the kid could take off and fly back to home base.This particular OX-5 had a nasty habit of dying without prior notice, a maneuver that sometimes had embarrassing consequences.  One morning the kid was helping  Norm start the OX-5. He swung the prop until he was exhausted but could get nothing for his efforts. Scotty, a B & M Airline mechanic, was doing some work on one of their tri-motors.

He noticed the difficulty and walked over.   "Having some problems?" he asked.  "Yes! and it's happening more and more all the time," answered Norm.  "Could be a magneto problem.   Sometimes vibration will jar the blocks loose from the wax-sealant and condensation will penetrate the magneto box and short the magnetos out,"  said Scotty.

The magnetos on the OX-5 Travelaire were mounted on top at the front of the engine, with no cover over them. Scotty pulled his stepladder over to the front of the airplane and removed the engine cowling. He unsnapped the magneto blocks and pulled them out.

"There's your problem," said Scotty, holding the blocks up, "The wax is gone. You need to get some wax and apply it in order to waterproof the blocks. But first you need to dry them," he said. Norm took the blocks into the shop, wiped them clean and dried them with a hair dryer. Meanwhile, the magneto box was cleaned and dried. They melted some wax, and once the blocks were reinstalled, the wax was applied under Scotty's supervision. Never had another problem with the OX-5 engine.

At the beginning of World War II, Norm returned to Canada to fly with the Royal Canadian Air Force. He never came back. But then, none of them returned to that area after the war. Those who survived the War, found other pursuits more rewarding. Before he left, Norm sold the airplane to a farmer named Bruce Dorsey who had a farm some where southeast of the airport. It was perhaps an hour away. Dorsey flew the airplane home where he promptly wrecked it for the final time. Seems like he was buzzing the farm at a low altitude and hit a water tank guy wire with a wing tip. He came away with a broken leg and some bruises.

Jack Howlett. manager of the Penney Store, bought a new, bright red Cub Coupe. He didn't have a license. No one else was around so he asked the kid to fly all his friends out around and over the town and back. The new Coupe had side by side seating arrangement and a wheel type control, a throttle on the instrument panel column instead of a stick between the knees and the throttle on the left wall.

The Coupe also incorporated a 65 hp Lycoming engine. Flying from early afternoon until nearly dark, the kid took a lot of Howlett's friends for a ride that day. The new Cub was a beautiful machine. It could crank out a higher speed than the other Cubs the kid had been flying.

Later, the kid flew a few prospective flight students on demonstration rides in the Cub. Handing them the controls usually convinced them they should be pilots. On one occasion, the kid had to persuade a terrified, potential student to let go of the controls by tapping him on the shoulder and showing him the fire extinguisher he was holding over his head. Upon the return to the field, the prospective student said: "I know I appeared to be real nervous on the outside up there, however, on the inside I was as cool as a cucumber." Some cucumber, the kid observed to himself.

Ernie was busy instructing students who ranged from young kids to middle aged business men and farmers. Most of the crop dusters had gone south for the winter to dust crops there. They would soon to begin the cycle of chasing the crops north.

Ernie, Matty and the kid were getting ready for winter. Cleaning out the wood burning heater in the office. Bringing down the skiis for installation on airplanes for the first snows. There had been some slight dusting with snow by some of the weather fronts common in late September and October.

The guys were also busy planning a trip to New York for Thanksgiving week. They were working on the big Stinson freighter getting it ready for the flight. The kid was back in school anticipating graduation in June.

# CHAPTER 10

## OPERATING AN AIRPORT AT AGE 17

Ernie and the other Island Crop Dusting Company guys usually flew home to New York for the holidays or on a charter flight to the World heavyweight fights with Joe Louis. When they did, in 1937, the year of his 17th birthday, they left the kid in charge of the airport which included the servicing operations, and care of several airplanes. Looking back, the kid thought he did a pretty good job with his limited brain capacity; however, two incidents occurred that are burned into his memory bank: Incident number one was the crash of a new Piper Cub by Jack Howlett, Manager of the local Penney store, Chamber of Commerce member, civic leader and an avid booster of local aviation.

The guys had gone to New York for the Thanksgiving holidays. They had left the usual strict instructions: no one was to fly their airplanes. The kid was to carry out the usual routines, answer the phones, service and pre-flight the airliner, and to call them in event of an emergency.

It was the day before Thanksgiving. The airliner had just left. The kid was in the office writing down some instructions Captain Bean had left for Ernie upon his return from New York. Jack Howlett suddenly appeared in the office doorway. "I'm flying the Cub down south to my sister's farm. I'll be back tomorrow afternoon," he announced. "Ernie left orders with me that no one was to fly Island Crop Dusting Company airplanes while he was gone." responded the kid.

Jack became extremely angry, something the kid had not seen in him before. He then proceeded to bully and then, completely out of character for him, he physically pushed the kid out of the way. He rolled the new yellow Piper J3 Cub out of the hangar.

Jack had just recently qualified for his Private Pilot's license and was still not, what the kid considered, blessed with an aptitude for flying. He took off down the east-west runway and climbed away from the field heading south.

The kid resisted the urge to call Ernie in New York. Why upset his holiday and well deserved rest? He spent a fitful night fighting a strange foreboding that something was about to go wrong. He felt that he should have resisted Jack more strongly.

Next day, still worried about the situation, as the day grew on and shadows began to lengthen, he was sure that somehow something bad had happened.

After sitting by the phone in the office all day, expecting bad news, he went outside to stretch his legs. He lit a cigarette and took one puff. Then it happened: the headlights of a large vehicle slowly entered the airport driveway confirming his worst fears. There on the back of a truck were the crumpled remains of the new yellow Cub.

It seems that when departing his sister's farm, Jack chose to perform a death defying stunt by attempting a downwind takeoff, heading into the foothills of a big mountain. The airplane, sucked into a down draft, pancaked onto the ground with full force. Even a pigeon knows it can't get off the ground with a downwind start. Miracles of miracles, except for minor injuries, jack was all right. But he sure had livened up the kid's life. While the kid called Ernie in New York, to report the accident, a very humble Jack volunteered to confess his bullying and hence the accident. When he offered to pay for repair of the airplane, Ernie forgave him.

Jack Howlett, Manager of the local JC Penney store, was a rabid booster of early aviation on the local scene. He was very active in civic affairs in the area, and whenever possible, he was a promoter of the kid's welfare.

Jack got the kid his first paying job, working with a government surveyor, held the survey rod for the Surveyor as he laid out the lines for installation of a range station, used for aerial navigation, which was built a long time afterward. Jack had learned to fly with Ernie and was quite frequently involved with promotions to benefit the airport. He quit flying after an accident.

Incident number two involved the crash of a Curtiss OX-5 Travelaire biplane owned locally by two characters known as the Poland brothers. A year earlier, while drunk, they had crashed into a huge Elm tree adjacent to the south side of the hangar. The younger of the two, Chester, never fully recovered from head injuries suffered when the tree contacted his skull while he sat in the front seat as his brother's passenger. He too was drunk. Somehow he was spared the memory of the crash. They both were a hard-drinking, fun loving pair; always pushing the limits of the safety envelope of whatever vehicle they were in at any given moment.

Ernie and the other Island Crop Dusting Company guys had gone to New York for the Christmas holidays. Before leaving, Ernie, along with the usual instructions, left special orders to prevent the brothers from removing the OX-5 Travelaire from the hangar. It seems they had not paid for repairs involved with rebuilding the airplane following their previous crash.

The Island Crop Dusting boys had only been gone a couple of days when Pat, the pilot and the oldest of the two Polands, arrived at the hangar ready to fly their airplane. Pat was big, mean and drunk. The kid relayed Ernie's orders: to which Pat said, "get out of my way and stay out or I'll knock your block off. I'm going to fly my airplane and, no one is going to stop me."

A heavy carpet of snow had been dumped on the ground by a storm a few days before. Snowplows had cleared the runways and the apron in front of the hangar. An unseasonably warm sun had reduced the snow into small puddles of water in front of the hangar. Over night the melted snow had refrozen, leaving ice in patches all over the ramp approaching the runway.

The Polands pushed the airplane out of the hangar. Once outside, the younger of the two, Chester, took off with their car, like a scared rabbit. Undisturbed, Pat reached into the cockpit and turned the switch on. He opened the throttle just a crack. The throttle arrangement on the Travelaire was a simple bellcrank design that easily opened and closed. In fact during flight, the pilot kept a hand constantly on the thing lest it either closed or opened by itself because of vibration.

Seeing that Pat could not be stopped, the kid offered to swing the propeller for him because he thought Pat was going to get killed if he pulled the propeller himself. "Git to hell away from me," Pat snarled, reaching unsteadily upward for the propeller.

The kid knew the routine Pat had in mind because he had seen others do it repeatedly without incident. Guys would open the throttle, turn on the switch, pull the propeller through. When the engine started, they ran around the airplane, grabbed the cockpit rim, and vaulted over the side cowboy style. Off they'd go flying down the runway and up into the blue.

Pat performed the maneuver flawlessly, with one exception; when the engine started, the airplane began to roll ahead (he had not chocked the wheels because he didn't even want the kid to pull the chocks). As he backed away from the propeller and lunged unsteadily toward the cockpit, he slipped on the ice.

As the airplane wing passed over his prone body, Pat let out a terrible howl. The airplane bounced down hill over the rough frozen ground, picking up momentum so rapidly Pat could not catch it. The kid watched, frozen in place, as the old biplane with the bright orange wings and sky blue fuselage roared down the runway, throttle jarred wide open. The engine was howling like a scalded "Banshee." And just like a giant bird, it lifted gracefully off the runway and began a long, steep climb to about 1500 feet. Slowly, ever so slowly, one wing dipped slightly, and suddenly the airplane did a perfect wingover, heading back toward the rear of the hangar, in a steep dive.

Pat took off running down the road towards town never to return to the scene of his crime. The kid ran past the hangar and dove into a ditch just in time to see the airplane hit the ground, just short of the hangar, throwing up a great wall of dirt that all but knocked the back out of the hangar. The old bird had died a fitting death; never again to majestically rise in flight as it had just done.

Needless to say, Ernie was upset when he found out. It's unknown if he ever got his money out of that job but he was grateful that the airplane stopped short of the hangar where all of his other birds were nesting.

A short time after the Island Crop Dusting boys returned from New York, they went into town for some hardware items. On the way back, as they came up over the crest of the hill, just below the airport, they saw the yellow tail section of a Cub airplane sticking up above the horizon across the highway from the airport. As they got closer their suspicions were confirmed.

It was indeed the Island Crop Dusting Company Cub. But what had happened? How did the thing get from the hangar to the nose down position in the potato field across the road?

The company guys had a routine when flying the Cub. On the taxi run back to the hangar the pilot reached down and turned off the fuel valve. The fuel starved engine usually shut down just as the airplane reached the ramp in front of the hangar. Then the pilot pulled the airplane back into the hangar, with the nose pointing out. Finally, the fuel valve was turned the back to the ON position and the switch was turned to the OFF position.

It seems that whoever flew the Cub last had neglected to turn switch to OFF  after it was parked in the hangar. Ernie's theory was, that in their absence some one fooling around the airplane, could have given the propeller a swing and the engine blasted away.  The airplane might have jumped the hangar doorsill, bounced across the ramp, out to the highway, became briefly airborne and nosed over into the field.

Someone later reported seeing a Ford mechanic that we knew only as "Frenchy" driving out of the airport just after the crash.  "Frenchy" was an artist with a welding torch. When confronted, he explained:  "All I did was look inside the Cub, stepped back, and then, as I walked past it to leave, I gave the propeller a yank and away the airplane went. It hit the ditch along side the driveway and bounced into the air. It gained altitude enough to clear the road and nose dived into the field. It scared hell out of me, so drove off."

The damage, however, was not major. It amounted to wing tip repairs and recovering, bent fuselage longerons and a new propeller.  They repaired the damage and re-covered the wings in the shop.  The kid learned helped rib stitch the wing fabric. Frenchy did the welding.

Applying Acetate primer dope to the wings was an experience never to be forgotten. The only ventilation in the shop was the front and rear doors. The day was hot and the fumes, although not obnoxious, were silently over- powering.

Nothing unusual was noticed until the guys began to giggle and the kid thought the whole thing was hilarious. Then they began throwing things at each other. Ernie heard the commotion in the office where he was doing some work on the books.  He ran over to the shop.  Luckily, he recognized what was happening and removed the guys to the outside air where they quickly recovered.

The wing panels were painted bright yellow with a black scalloped leading edge. The little Cub was beautiful. Multiple-coats of wax were rubbed in until the shine was like the Stinson Reliant with its 22 coats of paint and polish.

# CHAPTER 11

## BARNSTORMING IN THE NORTH COUNTRY

Late the next summer, the entire Company, except the kid, flew all the planes to Millinocket, Maine to perform as an Aerial Circus; with stunts, races, rides and parachute jumps. An advance man was sent out prior to the event to arrange posters, newspaper, and radio announcements. Stores were encouraged to provide tickets for free rides as a reward for spending a certain amount of money.

The kid had been left behind to watch the place, but not for long. The guys left on Friday; however, when they arrived, Vince Rideout, who was one of the company's students, called and asked the kid to bring his car down.

The kid drove all night and despite heavy early morning fog, arrived Saturday morning. The weather was clear and unlimited by the time he found the guys. The air was cool and crisp, and the crowd was already gathering. Excitement at the cow pasture near the edge of town had reached a fever pitch.

The kid's assignment was to keep the small fry and their curious parents from poking holes in the fabric and helping passengers in and out of the airplanes.

Big Herbie Noble was the barker. Herb was a big guy, gifted with a great voice. Perhaps he had been a sideshow barker somewhere with a traveling carnival. He was great, talking through all the stunt routines, and then when the crowd was at the fever pitch from all those loops, rolls, Immelmans, and wingovers that ended with a low level pass over the field, Herb began his pitch for rides; one price for a quick turn around the field for $2, another for a ride over the farm or house for $5, and yet another for a stunt ride at $10.

Regardless of who was flying the stunt routines, Herbie always attached a military rank to the name. For example, Ernie was always Captain Pretsch which turned out to be prophetic, as Ernie earned that title a few years later on a major airline.

All day long airplanes were constantly rolling out. The kid was busy running errands, refueling aircraft and with a hundred other chores. At day's end, they all walked uptown to a restaurant for dinner. After dinner, they scattered all over the town.

The kid was on his way to a movie when Ernie caught up with him. He handed the kid a roll of bills, a big roll. He told him to hang on to it. The kid stuck it in his jacket pocket and continued on the way to the movies. The movie was lousy so he left early for the hotel. At that time Millinocket was a Great Northern Paper Company mill town.

The hotel appeared to be more a dormitory than a hotel. Built entirely of wood, it looked like a big square box. The kid's room was complete with a "thunder mug" and in the closet was a big coil of rope with a huge iron hook attached. The sign on the back of the door read: "IN CASE OF FIRE, OPEN THE WINDOW AND INSTALL THE HOOK OVER THE SILL. LOWER THE ROPE TO THE GROUND AND SLIDE DOWN THE ROPE TO SAFETY."

If the fire happened to be underneath and coming up the wall, The kid imagined he was supposed to take off down the hall until he found a launching site on the opposite wall of the building. He flopped down on the bed and fell fast asleep. But in the middle of the night, he discovered why those things under the bed were called "thunder mugs," since all flooring in the hotel was made of squeaking boards.

The kid arose early and descended to the lobby. After a time, Ernie finally came down from his room. When everyone else arrived, they all went into the dining room for breakfast. Everyone was talking about the previous day's adventures, when suddenly Ernie said, "Who's got the money?" He had forgotten all about it and so had the kid. Clutching at his jacket pocket, he felt the roll still there. "Thank God!" he whispered to himself. The money was still there. He pulled the roll out from his pocket and handed it to Ernie. "How much is there?" asked Ernie. "I don't know," replied the kid. "Should be close to $600," said Herb Noble, "that's what I gave you, Ernie."

When Ernie got around to counting the roll, back at the home base, the figure was correct. The kid breathed a great sigh of relief. How easy it could have been to lose that roll. His jacket pockets were so shallow and he had been so careless. The air show and aerial circus events were repeated most weekends at the home airport until winter closed in.

It was rumored that Herbie Noble, the ex-carnival barker, had left home as a boy and had returned only briefly. He perhaps entered the military during World War II and never returned home after the war.  Many guys, including the kid, never went home after the war.  There was just no way to earn a living in the area.  Most employment was seasonal and not very lucrative.  Folks used to say that, in the  State of Maine, people raised kids for export.

The flight home was uneventful.  The kid flew home with Ernie.  Vince had taken his car and traveled south.  It was the first time the kid saw Mount Khatardin from the air, up close.  Snow was on the mountain top.  Winter was at hand and soon they would be back on skis hauling people and freight into the back country.

The following summer, the crew flew over to Prince Edward Island in Canada for more barnstorming.  The kid was away playing baseball in Quebec City so he missed out on a trip he always wanted to take.  Prince Edward Island is one of the most beautiful places on earth.

# CHAPTER 12

## BUSH FLYING IN THE GREAT NORTH WOODS

The Island Crop Dusting Company ran "bush flying" operations for logging companies into the back country of northwestern Maine and fishing and hunting parties. They were using the big Stinson freighter, two Curtiss Robins, a Stinson Reliant and a Waco cabin biplane on floats.

They also hauled fishing and hunting parties into the "Sporting Camps" established to house, feed, and guide "sports" (as they were called by the locals) from out of state, to the best hunting and fishing in the region. The "sports" would arrive with all kinds of fancy equipment from New York, Massachusetts and elsewhere.

They'd go back home with all kinds of fish and game without, in many cases, ever getting a line wet or firing a shot out of the fancy rifles they carried with them. All the old jokes we had heard about guides shooting game and hanging it in trees in anticipation of unsuccessful hunting safaris were somehow becoming unfunny.

Winter snows came early that year. At the beginning of November, the kid woke up on a Sunday morning to see a heavy blanket of snow over everything in sight. It was drifting deep, up to the window sills. Soon after breakfast he strapped on his skis and went up the hill to the airport. Ernie and Chick Raymond, a young farmer who sometimes took flying lessons, were already shoveling out the hangar doors.

They mounted skis on the big Stinson freighter. As a wheel was removed they slid the skis on the wheel hubs. When the skis were both mounted, they lowered the skis down on rollers (pipes) and pushed the big ship outside into the snow.

The skis were held in position, with the toe elevated, and secured by a bungee cord. As a safety precaution, a cable, the same length as the cord, was secured to the landing gear leg in the event the cord should break.

Ernie decided to flight test the ship so they started the big bird and moved out where the runway began, now buried in deep snow. He began the takeoff run. Halfway down the runway, they felt a thump, and the airplane shuddered. The airplane broke ground and lifted up out of the deep snow. A quick check revealed they had hit something buried in the snow. The right ski was hanging straight down on the safety cable.

After a short confab, it was decided that Chick would hang out of the window and grab the bungee cord and attempt to straighten up the ski. The kid would hold Chick by the legs. In the bitter cold, with the freezing blast from the propeller, Chick could only last for a few short minutes at a time. So he was unsuccessful in trying to grab the bungee cord and cable. After about 15 unsuccessful attempts to grab the cable, Ernie called it off. The kid pulled Chick back out of the window. He was nearly frozen stiff.

Ernie then decided to return to the runway and crash land the big airplane. First, he circled low over town, blasting the engine hoping that someone would notice their plight and call the ambulance and fire trucks in case they were needed. He even flew real low right down onto the main drag, but it was wasted effort. Most folks were home sitting in front of the warm fire. Those few who were out never looked up.

After several more passes, Ernie yelled to the kid: "Go the rear and lay face down on the floor! Hold on to the legs of the last seat along the aisle!" He then turned in on the approach and dropped the big ship down over the fence at the end of the runway, and then down gently into the deep powdery snow.

Ernie cut the switch and luckily, the big prop stopped straight across. Holding the airplane off the damaged ski, he slowed it down to where they were slowly floating. Then, gently, the tip of the ski, with the broken cable, dug into the frozen turf and flipped over. The airplane spun around with the right wing tip sliding over the snow like a toboggan. Very minor damage occurred and the big bird was back in the air in a couple of days.

Only a few days later, they were airborne, flying over a great winter wonderland of beautiful white carpeting. The destination was Big Fish Lake in the western part of the State, deep in the forest. On board the big Stinson was a party bound for ice fishing and the kid was invited along. He soon found out why.

One of the passengers, a heavy-set older man, had a heart problem and he had some pills. The kid was to carefully observe him at all times, and should he begin to make gasping noises and begin to turn blue, he was to place one of the pills, the man carried in his breast pocket, on the back of his tongue.

They arrived at Big Fish lake and landed without incident. Snow was quite deep on the lake and as the skis bobbed along over the snow and the rough surfaces where the snow had blown away, Ernie pulled a wrench from beneath his seat and handed to the kid. He yelled: "When we stop grab the oil bucket out of the baggage compartment, jump out and run to the front of the airplane. When the prop stops, remove the oil plug from the engine sump and drain the oil into the bucket before it congeals in this freezing temperature."

When the oil stopped draining, the kid ran to the cook's cabin with the bucket of hot oil and the cook put it behind the big range in the kitchen. As it turned out, the temperature was 40 degrees below zero. To make things worse, the kid never owned a heavy jacket until the Army gave him one in Italy during world war II.

Ernie had to get the ship back to home base next morning so he and the kid were up at the first blush of daylight. The temperature had dropped. The kid shivered uncontrollably as he took a plumber's pot out of the airplane's baggage compartment. After lighting the plumber's pot, and placing a stovepipe on top of it, they pulled the sleeve of the engine cover down over the stovepipe so the heat would circulate throughout the engine.

Starting an airplane out in sub-zero temperature, back in those days, was a group exercise in team work. They stationed a guy up on the step, mid-level with the engine nacelle, to crank the inertia starter. When he got to the peak cranking rpm, Ernie flashed the signal to the kid and he ran down the hill to the airplane and handed the bucket of hot oil to another guy who poured it into the oil tank. Ernie pulled the starter control and the engine started.

If the engine not started on the first try, they would have been, "dead in the water," as the saying goes. Ernie taxied out of the cove onto the lake and swung around into the wind. The big airplane, trailing a long wake of swirling snow, thundered down the lake and disappeared into the haze.

As it turned out, there was very little fishing, a lot of boozing and card playing. Thankfully, the old man never needed his pills after all. The kid was the only one who really did any fishing. He was so successful that all the others offered to purchase his "catch" but he steadfastly hung onto it. Those big trout were going to his Mom's kitchen and from there into the family's collective bellies.

Seth Yerrington picked us up at the end of the week. None of the "sports" had removed their clothes during their stay at the lake. The kid hadn't because he felt strongly that it would have been a good way to instantly freeze. On the way back, Seth let the kid fly the airplane while he went to the rear to talk to someone.

The old man with the pills had been sleeping. Waking up for a moment, he saw him at the controls of the big Stinson. He was so shocked that for many years after he never got tired of telling anyone who would listen about the time the little kid flew him out of the woods with the big airplane.

That year Ernie began hauling freight out to Chamberlain Lake for the Great Northern logging operations. Chamberlain Lake was about 100 miles west and slightly to the south. On one particular flight, the kid traveled with Ernie. After they unloaded the airplane, Great Northern sent Ernie to north to Fort Kent for an overnight load pick up. Ernie left the kid there at the lake.

The loggers spoke only French and the kid didn't. They were all trying to talk with him about the airplane he had come in with, but all he could do shrug his shoulders. Only one person in the big logging camp could speak both English and French fluently. She came to his rescue. So he got to carry on a conversation with real live loggers through an interpreter.

His rescuer was a beautiful young school marm who was married to the region's Game Warden whom she referred to only as Curly. She later wrote a book called, "Nine Mile Bridge." The story about her life as a school teacher in a logging camp and as a Game Warden's wife living in the "bush." She mentioned Ernie and Seth in the book. When Ernie returned the next day, he and the kid flew back to home base through heavy snow, bucking a "Noreaster" all the way.

Sometime later that winter, on a cold winter's night, Ernie got a desperate call to fly into Chamberlain Lake. They wanted him to pick up a young French Canadian logger who had nearly severed his foot at the ankle with an ax. The message was relayed via the border town up north because no direct telephone line, from the backwoods, existed.

The message was, in part: "Bad accident! Bring whiskey and haul him to the Fort Kent hospital!" Ernie took off, snow swirling out from behind the Curtiss Robin like a small tornado-whipped blizzard. The night was clear and as Matty and the kid watched, beneath a canopy of bright stars. They were awe stricken by the stark beauty of the night. They finally gave up and walked into the small office, at the corner of the hangar. They built a fire in the small, black, space heater, and settled down for the long wait.

There is no experience that can compare with the agonizing wait, by the ground crew, for a pilot to bring his bird back to roost. As a P-38 Crew Chief in World War II, the kid went through intense agony every time his pilot was out on a mission someplace over Europe. When the formation roared back over the Base, he could instantly pick out his airplane. He also learned to pray a lot.

Chamberlain Lake lay about 100 miles to the southwest, a little more than an hour's flying time over heavily forested terrain. With only a flashlight to track the compass and to eyeball the instrument panel, Ernie hit the lake like it was a bullseye on a shooting range. Loggers had built a huge bonfire out on the lake to guide him in. One hour later Ernie touched down on the lake.

The men carefully loaded the injured logger on board along with a company nurse. The logger was just a fuzzy-faced boy and this accident was the end of his first job. The nurse had applied a tourniquet to injured leg and took close care of him all the way to the hospital. Ernie took off hell bent for the little town of Fort Kent, about 90 miles to the north, bending the throttle all the way. Again the flashlight was used to navigate and watch the instruments. The boy was delirious and sobbed all the way to the hospital.

At the destination, the Fort Kent volunteer fire department had built a big bonfire on the river. Ernie flew straight in safely, although he had to fly under the bridge over the river, to a landing on the ice; no small feat even in the daylight. An ambulance was waiting to take the victim to the hospital where the boy's life and foot were saved, although it had been "nip and tuck" all the way.

Ernie walked up town to a telephone. He called the airport where they were waiting anxiously to hear that he had safely made it in to Fort Kent. "I'll be there in about an hour! Hang a lantern on the fence at the north end of the north-south runway!" he said.

Matty and the kid slogged out through the heavy snow, lit the lantern and hung it on the wire fence. They waited and watched, out in the bitter cold, for the familiar drone of the old Challenger engine. And after what seemed a lifetime, shortly after midnight, they heard the steady far-off drone of the engine and shortly thereafter, Ernie was back; touching the old Curtiss Robin down on the snow-packed runway, light as a feather.

That same year, The Island Crop Dusting Company contracted with Great Northern to fly all the loggers, who wanted to go, out to Fort Kent on the day before Christmas. Ernie left for Chamberlain Lake in early morning, on the target day, to begin the "Christmas-Home" operation. He was flying one of the Curtiss Robins.

The Robin was powered by a six cylinder engine, rated at 180 hp at full throttle. In August of 1930, a similar Challenger Robin broke the world endurance record, held by another Robin, at 647 hours, 28 minutes and 30 seconds.

PHOTO COURTESY E.C. SMITH

Ernie flew round trips between the lake and Fort Kent all day long, hauling four passengers per flight instead of the rated load limit of three. As darkness began to fall, and with three passengers already on board, Ernie announced:

"This trip will be the last flight for today. I'll return

69

early in the morning to pick up the rest of you." The two men who were to be left behind became extremely angry. Wielding axes over their heads, they screamed, "if we no fly today, no one fly. We break your machine."

Threatened with an attack if their demands were not met, and unable to speak their language, Ernie gave in. The seating arrangement in the Robin was not for five passengers and a pilot, but for a pilot in front in the single seat and two passengers in back on a bench-type seat.

Hijacked, under the threat of losing an airplane and being murdered by ax wielding loggers deep in the big forest, Ernie revised the seating arrangement: three men in the rear and three in the front, two men laying on the floor, one on each side of the pilot. These were not male midgets. They were heavy, rugged woodsmen who severely overloaded the half-hearted, tired old flying machine. It would take tremendous skill, strength and a full measure of luck to make it back to Fort Kent.

In spite of a strong headwind, the old Robin ran nearly a mile across the lake before staggering into the air. Once airborne, the tired old bird wallowed along at 200 feet altitude under full throttle. Long after darkness had settled over the country, they arrived at Fort Kent.

Volunteer Firemen had built a bonfire out on the ice. Landing, on the frozen river's surface, with only a bonfire to line up with, was a more precarious maneuver because of overloading and the necessity of flying in under the bridge, near the center of town, to a safe connection with the ice.

These flying feats were all the more remarkable, because there were no night flying instrumentation in the aircraft then, and no electronic navigational aids or other communication devices. Ernie had only a compass to guide him and a dim flashlight with which to read the compass and the four other instruments: tachometer, turn and bank indicator, oil temperature and pressure gauges. Of course he had the stars on clear nights.

After unloading his cargo, Ernie began to breathe easy again. Then, after the long hard day of flying, he headed for home and the lantern hanging on the fence. While Matty and the kid watched and waited, he again made it in safely touching down on the snow as soft as a feather.

Ernie and Seth flew several Fishing and hunting charters to far off Lakes, deep in the forests of northern

Maine. They always came back with game lashed to the pontoons.

Sproul had become an enigma around the Company by the end of that last dusting season. He would disappear then show up without warning, distance himself from the common folk in the hangar, chat with Ernie in the office, then disappear again always by automobile. Perhaps he sold his dusting airplane; never saw it again.

He came back one time with a Stinson passenger airplane and actually went out barnstorming with it. Somewhere, up along the northern border with Canada, he found a town named Escourt. He flew out of a hay field there on a Sunday afternoon hauling passengers. For some unknown reason, he walked off leaving the airplane unprotected in the field.

# CHAPTER 13

## PREPARING ERNIE FOR THE AIRLINES

In 1939 the kid went to Quebec, Canada to play baseball . Returning home at the end of the season, the kid discovered that the Island Crop Dusting Company had negotiated the acquisition of a Stinson "T" tri-motor from Boston and Maine Airline. Ernie wanted to equip himself for an airline job. He traveled to Boston on the airline with Captain Don Stewart at the controls. Since the Stinson"T" had no co-pilot arrangement in the cockpit, during the entire flight, Ernie stood behind Captain Stewart, memorizing every move the Captain made.

At the airline office in Boston, Ernie met with Clarence Belinn, Boston & Maine's Chief of Flight Operations. Belinn was an old crop duster and a former airmail pilot, flying the old Jenny biplane. They completed the deal for $1800. Belinn gave Ernie a Pilot's Operator's manual and the bill of sale. After a short conversation, during which Clarence briefed Ernie on some of the flight characteristics of the airplane, they went out to the ramp to perform an orientation flight .

On board, with Ernie looking over his shoulder, Clarence talked him through a complete cockpit check. With Ernie still standing behind him, Clarence started the engines and taxied out to the runway. He took off, made one quick trip around the field, talking Ernie through every move he made. Clarence landed the tri-motor, taxied back in, shut everything down, and got up from the pilot's seat. As he started back down through the cabin, leaving Ernie standing there, he said over his shoulder: "You're on your own. If you get in trouble, use the Operator's manual I gave you."

Ernie flew the tri-motor up to Bangor, Maine where he landed for refueling. He then flew all alone, in the big bird, to the northern-most airport in Maine. Ernie did a lot of flying to qualify for an instrument rating, one of the requirements for an Airline Pilot Certificate. The kid rode as a passenger on a couple of those flights. The Airliner was also taken out barnstorming and used in local air shows.

Awhile back, as the kid flew out from the east coast into Los Angeles, California, on board a Boeing 757. He made note of all the activity in the aisles: Stewardess' pushing carts of booze and food back and forth, people traveling to the rest rooms, and some standing in the aisles talking. He laid back in his seat and closed his eyes.

His thoughts returned to that old Stinson "T" back home at the airport in Caribou when Ernie was flying under the "hood" practicing for an instrument rating. The seat in the old airliner where the kid was sitting centered over the longeron where the wing struts hooked into the fuselage. The right outboard engine was partially secured on that strut. As a result, the seat was vibrating.

After about an hour of bouncing, his stomach began to feel a bit queasy. He got up and slipped into a seat to the rear by the baggage compartment. No sooner had he settled into the seat when Ernie yelled: "Who the hell moved back there? Get back to where you were! I just spent an hour trying to trim this thing for "hands off" flying." The kid hurried back to the seat he had just vacated. He felt so ashamed that he forgot about feeling queasy.

Ernie continued preparations for the Instrument Rating Test, using the Stinson Reliant, flying under the hood. He took the test with the FAA Inspector by flying him all the way to Boston under the hood. The inspector passed him and Ernie got his qualifying rating for the airlines.

Soon after applying to the airlines, Ernie sold the Island Crop Dusting Company and was hired by Transworld Airlines (TWA). Rumor had it that Clarence Sproul had bought the Island Crop Dusting Company. Ernie left for Kansas City and the Island Cop Dusting Company was gone. He flew on the airline as a Co-Pilot from 1939 to 1941 in Douglas DC-2 and DC-3 airplanes. He became a Captain in 1941 and was assigned to the Training Division of TWA and flew as check pilot until after World War II. He served in the U.S. Army Air Force Reserve from 1942 through 1946

In 1955 Ernie, along with 10 other check pilots, was loaned by TWA to Lufthansa Airlines in Germany. They were to raise the airline up from the of the rubble of war. Because Ernie could speak the language, he worked out of the Chief Pilot's office. In that position, he developed pilot training programs, planned, organized, and developed proving flights over the new international routes assigned to the airline.

With the loan of new Lockheed Constellations, pilots who hadn't flown an airline class airplane in more than 10 years, began training. Other personnel had to be trained also, and it wasn't long before the airline was up and running again.   Ernie flew many of the proving flights over the new routes.

He soon became the personal pilot of Germany's Chancellor, Konrad Adenaurer.   He flew the Chancellor all over the world.   Ernie spoke both French and German fluently which made him more valuable to the mission. Adenaurer liked to ride in the Co-Pilot's seat on all takeoffs and landings.  He flew the Chancellor on the historic mission to from Cologne, Germany to Moscow in the USSR where he was able to successfully negotiate the freedom of 10,000 German prisoners of war who had survived ten years in Soviet slave labor camps.

And in just five years, with Ernie's help, the airline took its place as one of the world's top quality airlines. Under his direction, Lufthansa Airline developed the best scheduled airline performance in the industry.  He returned in 1960 to TWA, which by that time, was known as Howard Hughes' airline.  Shortly after his return, he was assigned to fly all the paper boys of Chicago, along with Hopalong Cassidy, on a trip to Ireland.   The flight was made with the propeller-driven Lockheed Constellation airplane.  Upon his return to Kansas City from Ireland, the Boeing 707 was just coming on line and Ernie checked out in the new jet powered aircraft.

He flew as a Check Pilot for several years until 1969 when he checked out in the Boeing 747.  Soon thereafter, he was flying as a Captain on international routes to Europe where he broke five world speed records between London and New York and from Paris to Chicago. After a very colorful career, Ernie retired from airline flying in 1971. Ernie Pretsch was truly one of the "greats" in aviation.

After Ernie left the Island Crop Dusting Company, the kid often wondered if he missed those days with the Island Crop Dusting Company crew as he settled into the "hum-drum" life of an airline flyer where every move is choreographed according to a well ordered plan put together by experts.

He probably never had an occasion where people, like the cast of characters, known as the Island Crop Dusting Company, could keep his adrenaline flowing like a spring shower;  with their practical jokes and the shenanigans of visitors to the airport.  Of course the airline kept Ernie eating regular something he had not been able to do running his own company for one reason or another.

Following his retirement from the airlines, Ernie remained active in aviation until recently, as a Flight Examiner for the FAA in Florida. He now resides in Arizona with his wife Susan. At age 85 he is still flying his own airplane, a Cessna 182 that, perhaps has nearly as much instrumentation as the Boeing 747's he flew across the north Atlantic to Europe. As an ancient pilot, he now flies a lot with the Octogenarian Flyers Club of Arizona.

Ernie and wife Susan flew out to visit the kid in California a couple of years ago. The kid's friendship with Ernie spans more than 60 years, since 1935. And the kid still says that watching an airplane with Ernie at the controls is poetry in motion. Ernie Pretsch is one of the unknown "greats" in aviation history. He should of had the same press agent as some of the better known but lesser talents in the business. If he had connected with a press agent, he would have become famous. Perhaps he wouldn't have wanted that, but he certainly deserves it.

# CHAPTER 14

# TO NEW YORK CITY AND BACK

In 1938, with the coming of summer and no dusting contracts in sight, Matty Springer decided to go home to New York to visit his parents. He invited the kid to go with him. They were to leave on the fourth of July, however, a snow storm blanketed the area dropping two feet of wet snow on the country side. Since all snow removal equipment had been put in summer storage, they had to wait two days for the snow removal equipment to be removed from storage.

PHOTO COURTESY E.C. SMITH

They finally got off the ground early on the seventh of July. The local weather picture was clear with unlimited visibility, further to the south, weather conditions were vague. It called for some cloudiness, with high overcast at Roosevelt Field on Long Island, New York, their destination.

Matty was flying the Stinson Reliant. The Reliant was a classy airplane. It was powered with a 290 hp Lycoming engine that could push the airplane to 141 maximum airspeed. They were north of Bangor when the weather suddenly turned sour. Fog and low clouds dropped down all around them. Visibility was less than a half mile. Matty became momentarily disoriented. At one point, just north of Bangor, he cried out, "Get out the map and find a landmark of some kind." The kid grabbed the map. Off to the left he saw a fire warden's lookout tower. He was able to quickly locate it on the map. "We're just slightly east of the Penobscot River", he said.

Matty turned west 90 degrees and within minutes they were over the Penobscot river. He dropped down to where they were barely skimming the water. Suddenly, the kid remembered something he had read somewhere in the past: To keep abreast of the river current, many folks living along the Penobscot, had installed cables across the river. They tied up to the cable, as they poled their flat bottomed boats back and forth.

The kid told Matty to get a little more altitude, that there may be cables across the river. No sooner had he pulled the Stinson up, when there, beneath the right wing, a cable with a white rag attached went racing by with only a few feet to spare.

Shortly, thereafter, they broke out into high overcast with good visibility and flew on into the traffic pattern at Bangor. After a quick refueling, a visual check of the airplane, and a check of the weather conditions down the line, they were on the way again.

Somewhere south of Bangor they came out of the high overcast and visibility was good. Reaching Long Island Sound on the Connecticut side, however, they had to climb up over a thick layer of clouds out on the long Island Sound. Over Roosevelt Field, their destination, a thin cloud layer enabled Matty to peel down into the traffic pattern. Squaring out into the pattern, they beheld a strange sight. People, thousands of them, swarming like ants, were rushing out onto the field to surround a twin engine airplane that was trying to taxi in from the landing strip.

They were then diverted to Floyd Bennett Field. There, they found out that the excitement at Roosevelt was caused by the arrival of Howard Hughes and crew back from their flight around the world. Matty called his father, who was president of one of New York's boroughs. He came and picked them up. When they arrived at the Springer home the first words from Mr. Springer were, all in one breath, "Welcome to New York. We like boys from your State here in

New York. They are honest and they work hard. Which do you want, the fire department or the cops?"

The kid explained: "I appreciate the offer but I'm only 17 years old and still in high school." Next day they went to the city where the kid spent a whole awe-struck day gawking at the big buildings and the raging traffic. The kid saw what was supposed to be Grover Alexander and his flea circus, Primo Canero on the street and Jack Dempsey going into his restaurant. Next day it was Coney Island, something he could not really comprehend. He had nothing in his experience to relate to it.

Matty and his girl friend and another couple took the kid to Coney Island. They rode the Cyclone, the world's greatest roller coaster and they then went to a German Hofbrau where they gorged themselves on miniature sandwiches and brew. No one asked to see his identification.

The kid became fascinated with the fact that the blonde across the table from him was a brown eyed blonde. Back home, the only blondes he knew were blue eyed Swedes from the Colony of New Sweden near his home town. He hadn't been told about women dying their hair.

After a week in all that hustle and bustle, the impersonal attitude people had for each other, the unsmiling mob scene, and "superior" people, he was glad to leave for the tiny village in the north where he was on a first name relation with everyone in town including their dogs and cats.

# CHAPTER 15

# THE ESCOURT CAPER

One evening in 1938, the day before Thanksgiving, the kid got a call from a farmer who had been taking flying lessons from Ernie before he left for the airlines. He told the kid that Clarence Sproul had left his airplane in Escourt, Maine and he, the farmer, had to get it out before the snows came.

Escourt was about 134 miles northwest and is the northern-most spot in Maine. It is accessible only by driving up through Canada, traveling west, then back down through the Maine border into Escourt. Many folks think that Escourt's inclusion in the United States was a "goof" by Webster when he surveyed the Maine/Canadian borders during the last century. At any rate it has always been a problem to those who live in that area.

The farmer asked the kid to help him retrieve the airplane. Sproul was away from the area at the time and the kid had no way of knowing that Sproul was not involved in the airplane retrieval operation. Turns out Mr. Sproul had abandoned the airplane right where he had parked it earlier that summer. The reasons for such an act, involving a perfectly sound aircraft, were known only by God and Mr. Sproul.

The farmer was tall, lean and blessed with great strength; and he would need all the strength he could muster before the day was done. He arrived to pick the kid up at the ungodly hour of four in the morning. Thus they embarked on the strangest saga in which the kid has ever been involved; barring none. First off, he had never checked to see what the weather was going to be because, as they found out later, approaching the north country was one of the worst blizzards ever to hit the area.

The kid had not eaten breakfast because he assumed that the farmer would stop someplace to eat. He didn't. In fact he didn't ever stop anywhere, except in Escourt to dismantle, load and unload the airplane at the airport in Caribou and again, when they were back in front of the kid's house, sometime after midnight. Not only did he not stop at a restaurant, he brought no food with him.

They arrived in Escourt late in the morning, and by the time they found the airplane, a light snow was falling. The farmer quickly backed the truck up to the airplane, located in a pasture. First thing they did was to install chains on the old, beat up truck. Then, began the dismal task of dismantling the airplane. They were constantly hampered by heavy snow, driven by a 35 mph wind, that was now beginning to drive the snow horizontally.

Removing the wing struts was tough; the kid had to hold the wing tips while the farmer removed the bolts attaching the struts to the fuselage. The kid was still holding the wing tips, despite, heavy wind pressure, while the farmer removed the bolts holding the wings to the fuselage. They stowed the wings, leading edge down, along both sides of the truck bed. They then slid the struts behind the wings. The truck bed was sided with boards and stakes that were about six feet high.

Shivering in the cold, a long way from home, the kid's hands were frozen stiff. The kid had no gloves or mittens. Using a wrench and pulling out bolts with bare hands was sheer torture. He began to think of home and wondered if he'd ever see it again, and hoped that his Mom would save some thanksgiving dinner for him.

Using the hoist on the truck bed, the fuselage, complete with wheels, engine and propeller, was lifted onto the flatbed. They pushed it ahead to the truck cab. By the time they finished loading, the field was covered with at least a foot of snow. They secured the airplane with a rope.

The old truck had a tough time getting out of the field, slipping and sliding all over the place until they finally moved out onto the highway which was now covered with a blanket of trackless snow. A harbinger of troubles to come? No one was moving on the road which was also the main street of Escourt. The kid shivered way down in his shoes.

Only one time after that was the kid ever as cold or colder. It was on a Christmas eve while hundreds of troops were trying to sleep on the bare ground, in sub-zero weather, in Italy during World War II. It was so cold that any copy of the New York Times (preferably the Sunday edition), which would be used as insulation between body and earth, could bring the owner, someone just off the boat from the States, as much as ten dollars. At the time, an old Sergeant watching the kid shiver, said: "You might as well relax son, it ain't gonna git no warmer than this."

With the front wheels of the truck barely touching the road, from the heavy load on board, they began the long trek back to the airport in Caribou. The road ahead was buried. The windshield wipers were barely moving, straining against the snow. Lucky for them the snow was not wet, but was light and billowy.

As they picked up speed to a slow trot, had it been a horse, the wind buffeted the truck, and the front end swayed back and forth. The kid had the distinct feeling that even without a load the old truck would be swaying. To make matters worse, the road to the Maine border was unpaved, full of ruts and pot holes and nearly 70 miles away.

The farmer was continually struggling to get out and stay out of the ruts. He never spoke. However, they had made pretty good progress in some places, until they came to a long, steep grade. By now, the truck fenders were pushing the snow aside like a snowplow. The truck was slowly lurching along toward the summit.

Near the top of the grade, the truck suddenly stalled. It began to roll backwards. When the farmer applied the brakes, the truck slowly slid off the road into the ditch. As if watching a moving picture in slow motion, the tail section of the airplane rolled up into a bank lined with trees. Miraculously, no damage occurred except to the windshield fairing. A large nail protruding from the truck bed wall punctured the fairing. At this point they had covered about 50 miles in 3 hours.

Now, they were stuck, a long way from home and in the middle of the biggest blizzard to hit the area in years. Like all good farmers of that time, however, this guy had a sharp ax in the truck so they began to gather fir boughs to shove under the rear wheels. The biggest fear, at the moment, was that no one would discover their frozen bodies until spring.

After a lot of wheel spinning and some further sliding, the fir boughs finally worked, much to their surprise. The rear wheels gained traction and once more they inched along to the top of the summit. Though, the Angel of mercy must have been with them all through that long day.

Darkness had settled in, dropping down around them, like a great black blanket. It was snowing even harder, and rapidly building into one of the worst blizzards of all time. The kid couldn't see out of the windshield and for the life of him, he could not begin to imagine how the farmer was driving on the road so well. In retrospect, perhaps he wasn't always on the road.

Slowly, the truck crept over the top of the big hill making agonizing progress. Finally, over the crest they went, plunging down the other side, rapidly picking up speed. Snow was drifting in the road ahead. Going down hill they hit some fairly large drifts really hard. Snow was exploding all around them.

The kid prayed hard all the way to bottom that the farmer would not have to hit the brakes. Lucky for them, they met no other vehicles. Obviously, they were the only fools abroad that day. They passed through the border back into Maine with about 65 miles still in front of them to the airport and home.

The border agent expressed disbelief at what he saw approaching him: "You guys are crazy to be out on a night like this," he said. "They closed that road to all cars and trucks early this afternoon and it will stay closed until spring. You're lucky to get this far and the road south will not be any picnic for you either. Good luck!" Of course they had no way of knowing the road had been closed, for there was no radio in the truck.

The hunger pangs, the kid had suffered all day long, had given way, to a nagging fear of being stranded somewhere and freezing to death. As a matter of fact, as the border guard had told them, they were the last motor vehicle over the road, north of the border, until spring. People in that part of the country used horses and sleighs with which to travel during the winter months.

The snowplows were out on Highway 1, so they were able to make better time. They arrived back at the airport shortly after midnight. The kid rolled back the big hangar doors and the farmer backed the truck through the opening to the back of the hangar. They unloaded the airplane. Very carefully they stacked the wings against the back wall of the hangar. The farmer hoisted the fuselage off the truck and they pushed it into a corner. After securing the airplane and its major components, they closed the hangar doors and headed for home.

By the time the kid got into bed, it had been nearly 24 hours to the minute, from the time he had left his warm bed. His folks never even knew where he had gone, inasmuch as it had been a custom for him to disappear for short periods of time since The Island Crop Dusting Company had arrived at the airport.   His Mother did save some of her old fashioned Thanksgiving turkey for him.  But at that moment, a warm bed seemed more to his liking.

The farmer never gave him a dime, or thanked him, nor had he even thought of food.   Many of the folks, during that period, were used to short rations and the farmer was no exception.   At least he didn't appear to be afflicted with obesity.
Restaurants held no great attraction for many so perhaps it was not in his thought process to belly up to some lunch counter.

The farmer did seem to think that, although the Island Crop Dusting Company had ceased to exist and everyone had gone south,  the kid was somehow on the payroll of the company and therefore it was his solemn duty to help him. What he never knew was, the kid had worked only for flying time not for cash.  This was an arrangement that he liked much better because with money it's gone in a flash but things learned stay forever.

One day, just before leaving for Boston and the Army, late in the summer following the rescue of the airplane from Escourt, the kid happened to be at the airport hangar for some unknown reason.   Mr. Sproul, the owner of the abandoned airplane, had arrived.   He was surveying the airplane, accompanied by Freddie Flake.

As the kid walked over to where they were standing, it so happened at that precise moment, Freddie was pointing to the hole in the windshield fairing.  He was commenting about kids, meaning Matty and the kid, shooting .22 caliber rifles in the hangar, which no one had ever done.  The jerk was by now eyeballing the kid.  Sproul finally caught his eye and turned his head in that direction.  He saw the kid standing there.

Charging at him, like an enraged bull, he was mouthing a scathing string of obscenities.    Instead of expressing his gratitude for saving his airplane, he  bellowed: "Who in hell authorized you to remove this airplane?   Get to hell off this airport right now.  If I ever catch you around here again, I'll kick your butt all over this field."

Although the kid doubted very strongly that Sproul could, or would attempt to carry out the threats, he left never to return or even look back.  The hole in the windshield fairing was of course made, not by Matty or the kid shooting guns at airplanes in the hangar, but by a large nail protruding from the wall board on the truck bed, made during the journey from Escourt.

Nor were there any bullet holes in the wall of the hangar as an indication of someone shooting from outside. Had it been a bullet, the windshield would have been shattered. But Mr. Sproul never let the kid explain, much less tell him the real story.

Again, why did a supposedly intelligent, educated man leave a perfectly sound airplane to face certain destruction by the gale forces of weather during a long, severe northern winter. The ship wasn't even secured to the ground by tie-downs. Why was he so angry at the rescue? We will never know.

Clarence Sproul was a good pilot. In early 1942, the kid caught a glimpse of Sproul in a newsreel at a movie theater on France Field in Panama. He was flying the north Atlantic with Winston Churchill as a passenger. They were flying in a Lockheed Hudson. Sproul will always be remembered, but in a negative way.

# CHAPTER 16

# SOME INTERESTING EVENTS AND CHARACTERS

There has always been a special bond, a brotherhood, or an unwritten chivalry code, of some sort, between flyers the world over. There were stories coming from World War I about malfunctioning aircraft escaping fire through the courtesy of an enemy pilot. Other stories were often told of special treatment for downed fliers behind enemy lines during the War. This mutual respect appeared to extend beyond cultural and political boundaries.

On a gray day in October 1938, rain or snow threatened to engulf the land, so it was a down day as far as flying went. They were all in the office listening to music on the old Atwater Kent radio when suddenly there was an announcement about two Russians pilots who were flying the Atlantic to New York and the World's Fair. According to the announcement, they were overdue by several hours. Northern Maine is not far from Newfoundland and it was conceivable that they could be down somewhere in Eastern Maine or in New Brunswick, Canada. They all were instantly galvanized with anxiety.

Even though he had no love for Communists, Ernie lost no time in going out to search near the coast of New Brunswick for the lost Russian Pilots who had failed the Paris to USA route via the Atlantic Ocean; Loitering in the area long enough to confirm that the Russians were not on the ground, Ernie was forced to turn back to home base because the coast was "socked in" with pea soup fog.

Back in the office, the crew cranked up the old Atwater Kent radio and listened anxiously for any word that would tell them the pilots were safe. But on that day, for Ernie, there were only other pilots lost out there somewhere; no nationalities were involved. No trace of the lost fliers was ever discovered.

Fred Anderson was a frequent airport visitor flying an ancient vintage airplane that no one is familiar with today. He was all Swede, from his white hair to his speech and good looks. He flew that old airplane all over the country, a modern day Viking. Fred always sent the kid a postcard from where ever he went during his many flying trips around the country;

always offering words of encouragement. Fred died in combat flying a B-24 for Uncle Sam in World War II.

Merle Libby was a farmer with a perennial sunburn. He really didn't like farming; rather be fishing and hunting. So good was he at fishing, it was rumored that fishing buffs throughout the county tried following him to discover the best fishing areas. They were unsuccessful. He used every excuse in the book to run off somewhere fishing or hunting.

After Ernie taught him to fly, Merle bought an Aeronca, a small two-place airplane. Merle would fly that single engine airplane across the vast wilderness of Maine, New Brunswick and Newfoundland, to the north shore of the Saint Lawrence river, in both winter and summer. Had he gone down in that wilderness, No one would ever have found him.

When the call of the wild came over him, he would sometimes leave machinery and equipment in the fields, run to the house, grab a few things, run out to the plane and take off. Neighbors would put his equipment away. They knew that under the spell, Merle might be gone for a month or longer. Everyone said Merle should have been born an Indian.

Ernie taught two brothers, of French Canadian descent, to fly. Although they owned a successful car dealership, up north near the Maine-Canadian border, they could never agree on anything. They continually argued about everything under the sun.

They bought a single seat Aeronca airplane with side by side dual controls. So it came to pass that one day, on the way home from a flight, they got into a fight over who was going to land the airplane. Each one was determined to wrest the controls from the other. At that particular point they were on the approach to a field that had a big reservoir pond just below a sharp drop off in the land, at the end of the strip they were heading into.

They wound up on the ground rolling at full landing speed towards the drop off and the pond. Still fighting over the controls. But lucky for them, they ended up unhurt, caught between two trees on the edge of the hill overlooking the water. No damage was done to the fuselage, only the wings were heavily damaged. The Island Crop Dusting Company repaired the airplane.

State Trooper, Bert Robertson was a friend of Lew Howard and a fellow State Highway officer. The kid will never forget big Bert, tall, curly headed and handsome. By any definition, Bert was reckless. He constantly danced with death in speeding cars on roads built for Model T Fords from which the thrill, however perverse, somehow fascinated him beyond control. He learned to fly, taking lessons at the Island Crop Dusting Company's Flight School.

Bert died in a flying accident only a few miles from where he learned to fly. He was flying an Army Air Corps A-26, a most difficult airplane to fly. He was buzzing a potato farm in northern Maine on his way to the war in Europe and smashed into the ground. The resulting death toll included several farm workers. It was his wife's birthplace and she witnessed the crash.

The kid will never forget Barbara Morgan. She was a cute little girl who lived across the street from his home. She grew up to be a beautiful young lady and he never even noticed. At their fortieth high school class reunion in 1977, the kid met Barbara. She and her husband invited he and his wife to their home after the festivities of the day had ended.

Over coffee and cakes she told a little story about the kid's rabid interest in airplanes back in the "thirties." One day she had complained to her mother: "Mom, I've done everything but hit him on the head but he doesn't even know I'm alive." Her mother answered: "Barb! Unfortunately for you, he discovered airplanes first." And so he had.

In the summer of 1939, the kid's father was dying. No doctor would come to the house because they were unsure of the bill being paid. He suffered terribly for a long time. The family had no car at the time but they could ride the train on a pass. That was one of the few benefits he received from his employment on the railroad.

Any other railroad benefits he had to show for more than 30 years of excellent service escaped the rational mind. Grandma always said that railroading wasn't a job, it was a disease, which perhaps explained dad's devotion to the job.

The kid's mother decided to secure a pass and send his little sister by train to Grandma, who lived 60 miles to the south, to escape the agony of Father's condition. But after a couple of weeks, dad began to ask for Betty. At the time, the family had no transportation, except the kid had access to the Cub.

The kid borrowed the Cub for the short flight south to pick up little sister. The day was beautiful. A slight breeze from the northwest was stirring the leaves as he lifted the small Cub off the runway. He headed south and after about 50 minutes, arrived at the airport in Houlton, Maine where his Grandmother lived.

He walked the two miles to her house. Grandpa had died a few years earlier and Grandma had recently remarried to a railroad man. She had then moved to his home. They packed up Betty's things and Grandma drove them to the airport. Before take off, he asked little sister if she needed to go to the restroom. She just shrugged her shoulders and said, "No!"

They lifted off the runway, climbed out of the traffic pattern heading north. Typical of many females, of one kind or another, under locomotion, his sister began to whimper about the need to go "potty" as she put it. He stubbornly told her to "hold it!" It's bad enough to make frequent "pit stops" for the female gender when driving an automobile. One only has to find a service station and whip off the highway, but it's quite another situation when flying an airplane. First you had to set down in a safe place.

Once a place was found no bushes were big enough to hide from the crowd that always appeared, instantly, the minute an airplane touched down any place. So he kept telling her to wait and she kept whimpering which, by then, was much more of a wail than a whimper.

In due time Presque Isle appeared on the horizon. He dropped the little bird down onto the runway and taxied quickly to the hangar. The airport appeared to be in a sad state of disrepair, more associated with abandonment than poor maintenance.

Reaching the hangar, he helped little sister out of the rear seat and off she ran to what had once been a rest room offering now more cover than comfort. So she "peed" on the cement floor and all over her Keds.

They cleared the runway, and again she began to whimper about going to the rest room. This time he successfully fought her off and they returned to good old home town terra firma as dry as unbuttered popcorn. His dad was pleased to see Betty and it turned out to be the last time for him, because he lapsed into a semi-coma which lasted until he passed on some time later.

The kid had one more flight to make though. Betty had gone to a lake, camping with her Brownie troop. A few days after she left, dad passed on. The kid had been sitting up with him nights. On the night of his passing, he suddenly became conscious of what was going on and began to speak. He said: "Why don't you get out for a rest. Go to a movie or something." So the kid went out for awhile but when he came back up the street, from a distance, he could see that the house was surrounded by cars. And he knew that his Father had gone.

Once again little sister Betty had to be picked up. The kid tried several places to borrow a car or just a ride to the lake but no one was able to spare the time or a car. So he borrowed the Cub again, tanked up five gallons of unpaid gasoline and rode off into the wild blue yonder to again pick up little sister.

Arriving at the lake in late afternoon, he circled the area searching for a suitable landing spot near the lake, since the nearby town had no airport. Finally, he saw a dirt road that partially circled the lake. There appeared to be a short stretch with room enough to land if he slipped the Cub hard into it.

There were no flaps or brakes on any of the older Island Crop Dusting Company equipment. The later semi-gull winged model Stinson Reliant had brakes, but no flaps. The Cub rolled out to the end of the strip he had selected. He shut down the engine, and pushed the little bird off the road out of the way of traffic.

After an hour of walking and searching for his little sister, he stumbled into a sea of small green pup tents in a field. He found little sister busy with some sort of craft that looked like something out of the ancient past, a beaded leather strap. As they walked back to the airplane, Betty kept asking why she had to give up camping. He couldn't bring himself to tell her. So he strapped her, kicking and howling, into the back seat of the Cub.

The little Cub climbed off the road heading east. Once again sister began to whimper that she had to go. He stalled her until an airport halfway home appeared on the horizon. They touched down on the runway and taxied quickly to the hangar. Betty disappeared and soon came sprinting back to the airplane.

No sooner had they become airborne again, when she began to whimper again. The kid said, "you just went!" She answered, "No I didn't." He asked, "why not?" She said, "I didn't need to go "Why did you lie to me?" he asked. "Because it's so much fun to land and take-off," she said. "I'm not stopping until we're home!" he snapped. And they didn't.    They landed at the home airport and taxied to the hangar, shut down the engine, and pushed the Cub inside the hangar. The kid asked, "why don't you go potty now?" She whined, "I'm too angry."

Late that summer, on one of those days built for flying,   the kid fired up the Cub and took off on a barnstorming cruise to an area about 70 miles southwest of the airport.    Before taking off, he removed the exhaust collector, and installed the short stacks.   The extra noise would attract more people as he buzzed the town. After a few passes over the small town, he dropped the Cub down on a strip of clover along side the highway, in a sparsely settled area, at the edge of the town. He taxied back up to the end of the strip, shut the engine down and waited.  Didn't have long to wait before a crowd began to gather and soon he was doing a land office business collecting fuel money to pay for the flight.

Because of the heavy wintertime snows, farmers in the area built their houses close to the highways and their barns were located to the rear of the houses.  Most houses had radio aerials on the rooftops which were constructed of piano wire stretching from the top of the house back to the top of the barn.  The wire was held in place by vertical strips of wood nailed to the barn's ridge poles.

The clover strip, the kid had landed on, lined up perfectly with the space between the houses and the barns for the entire length of the populated area. The day was calm and clover was tall which combined to make take-off difficult. The little Cub was laboring mightily on one particular trip, even at nearly full throttle.

Suddenly, the kid felt a tugging motion from tail section.  Looking back over his shoulder, he saw a long length of someone's radio aerial whipping around with shingles flying off the rooftop in all directions.  One of the rooftop aerial cables had hooked onto the tail skid.

Later on towards evening, with the sun sinking into the hills, a huge farmer, wearing bib overalls, approached the Cub at the end of a run. He asked if the kid would haul him out over his farm house so he could see what it looked like from the air. From the looks of him, he must of weighed over three hundred pounds which greatly exceeded the load limits for the J2 cub. He barely squeezed down into the rear seat.

They began the take-off run but couldn't get the tail off the ground. Since the kid was determined that the man was going to see his home from the sky, he ran the Cub back and forth across the strip until the tail came up and they began to get up some speed.

The end of the field, on the take-off run, was divided from the next field by a mound of rocks piled about six feet high. This mound of rocks had a thicket of green weed trees of doubtful origin reaching for the sky to a height of ten feet.

The point of no return was passed and they still couldn't get over the trees, so the kid flew right on through them and across the next field without gaining any altitude. The river was off to the right so he made a slewing, flat turn under the electric wires to the other side of the road. The little Cub wallowed out over the river bank. Why the little bird didn't stall and spin in, no one will never know. But about halfway across the river, they caught a sizable updraft and gained maneuvering altitude.

He flew over the man's house and he was extremely happy. Said the kid was as good a pilot as Charlie Lindbergh. Such ignorance was as much bliss, back then, as it is today. Little did he know how close they had come to making a trip to that great airport in the clouds, piloted by a complete novice.

The adventures for that day had come to an end. And the kid headed for home in the fading light of another great day in the life of a "good as Lindbergh" novice pilot who had a lot to learn about the laws of aerodynamics and other things. More than that, he learned with each passing incident, that his ears were symbolically growing longer until he now had the demeanor of the Jackass.

# CHAPTER 17

## YOU 'RE IN THE ARMY NOW

With The Island Crop Dusting Company now history, life had to go on. War clouds were looming in Europe. Hitler had invaded Poland. Beanie, who was also a US Army Air Corps Reserve pilot, and others, had been giving the kid advice about serving in the military. Now that the draft was a foregone conclusion, it was determined that an enlistment, at that point, could result in entry to the desired branch of service. The kid's first choice was the air arm of the US Marine Corps.

Matty had moved to Boston to prepare for an instrument rating to go with his commercial license. He had asked the kid to come down and spend some time with him. So he traveled to Boston and subsequently enlisted in the Marines. They gave him the required physical and dismissed him with the order to come back in a week for a re-physical examination. Two days later, he had a toothache. To have the tooth filled cost eight dollars. To have it pulled cost two dollars. He had five dollars to his name so the tooth came out.

When the time came for the re-physical, the kid said good-bye to Matty. He caught a bus to the Boston Marine recruiting office. Prior to the re-examination, the doctor, asked a few questions about any matters of health that might have occurred during the week. The kid told him about the tooth, whereupon, he was rejected because he didn't have the required number of molars. In the doctor's words: "Marines must be able to eat raw meat and for that you need all your molars." The kid didn't argue the point. Instead, he went down the street to the US Army Air Corps, where he really belonged, and was accepted, without hesitation, for a two year hitch.

From Boston he was shipped by train to New Rochelle and by ferry boat to Fort Slocum where the Army had just decided that Air Corps troops were too soft. Infantry officers decided that mechanics needed hand to hand combat training to cope with the rigors of maintaining a tool box.

The kid's group were the only victims of the misguided tactic designed more from envy than common sense.  At any rate, the program was a dismal failure.  The kid still chuckles over the antics of a Drill Instructor who stuck his jaw against the kid's face and yelled: "I'll break your spirit if it's the last thing I ever do."  Perhaps it was the kid's stoic nature that drove him mad.

The first pass he got to go into New York City was his last.  Two women, on separate occasions, spit in his face.  The first happened while he was standing in a line waiting to go inside a theater to a movie.  A woman coming out leaned over the dividing rope and spit right in his face.  A Red Cross lady, standing nearby, came running over and wiped the stuff off his face and apologized for the barbarian who did the spitting.

The second time it happened he was on the way into a restaurant.  He held the door for a woman coming out.  She splattered it all over his face.  The kid had never before encountered such hatred.  And he thought he had done something patriotic by enlisting.  Something to be proud about.

From Fort Slocum he and his new found buddies were hauled down the river on a barge to the Brooklyn Army Base.  The area was called the combat zone because outside the gate, recruits were routinely assaulted by street gangs.  A couple of recruits were murdered on the street in front of the Base.

The Base Commander advised that anyone wanting a pass badly enough to brave the existing situation, should go out in pairs.  It was only when a young recruit was alone that the gangs were brave enough to attack.  The kid never went outside or back to New York City, mindful of the hatred there.

All the recruits "sweated" the shipping lists, eagerly hoping for some tropical paradise where lots of flying was going on.  On the day after Thanksgiving, they sailed out from Brooklyn aboard a rusty old bucket, named the San Mihiel, bound for the Philippines.  However, the ship stopped at Cristobal in the Panama Canal Zone.  The kid was taken from the ship and driven in a staff car by a Major to France Field, near Coco Solo.

Thinking something may have happened to his mother, the kid asked the Major where they were going and why.  He didn't answer.  He appeared to be extremely agitated, perhaps because he was chauffeuring an enlisted man, a clear violation of the Army caste system.  They arrived at a base, which had been a United States Naval Seaplane Station.

The Major ushered him into the Base Commander's office. The commander was a rather short, rotund Colonel, who looked more like someone's doting grandfather than a West Point graduate. He grabbed the kid's hand before he had a chance to salute and enthusiastically greeted him as if he was a long lost son. He made a short speech, in which he basically said: "Young man, welcome to France Field. You are the forerunner of a great athletic program we are building here."

It seems that the Colonel had a "hook" in the Adjutant General's Office in Washington, D. C. who was to check all the records on recent enlistments for athletes. Since the kid had reported his last employment as a baseball player in the Provincial League in Quebec, he had been "speared" for France Field in the Canal Zone in Panama. "You're the first," he said. " We've never won a baseball game in our sector, so we expect great things of you," he added. The season was about to begin.

Now, the kid had enlisted to work on and be around airplanes which were his undying passion. He didn't go to all that trouble just to play baseball. His sights were now on aviation; but he settled into his situation, took the idea in stride. He had been told that his hardest job was to go to the gym in the mornings, work out and attend baseball practice.

The season began. In his first outing, the kid struck out 24 batters. He really felt bad about it because most of them were kids who had little experience. That whole season was similar. The Colonel was delirious with excitement and lamented the rules that prohibited him from buying the kid a beer at the officer's club. He right then and there decided that the kid should become an officer.

The kid was getting a lot of publicity in the Panamanian press. At the Colonel's urging, he applied for Officer's Candidate school. At the interview with the board who screened applicants, he was asked why he wanted to become an officer. The kid answered, "because the Colonel wants me to become an officer."

The interviewer replied: "That's all Sergeant! You are dismissed. That's not the proper reason for wanting to become an officer in the US Army Air Corps." The Colonel never brought the subject up again.

As anyone, who was there, can attest, during that period, Apartheid not only applied to blacks but, as far as the white civilian populace was concerned, of whom many were ex-military, it applied to the active military white boys.

Drinking fountains and rest rooms were labeled gold and silver. The silver applied to blacks. There were separate facilities like restaurants and stores. Ball parks had separate bleachers. In the kid's case, he could play baseball with the Canal Zone folk, but they would not so much as acknowledge his existence off the field.

Nearly a year had gone by and major League scouts were getting excited. He got several offers from major league clubs who had scouted his performance in the winter league where several major and minor leaguers were playing.

Out of the blue, came a call one day from a man in Panama, who at that time, was the equivalent of a Senator in the United States legislative branch of government. He requested a meeting with the kid. Of course the kid agreed. Acting upon the directions the man provided, the kid appeared at his address and was immediately ushered into the inner sanctum. The Panamanian politician was a personable man, with the biggest smile the kid had ever seen in his life. He motioned to a chair and the kid sat down bursting with curiosity. He spoke: "Panama is entering the Central American Baseball League. We have just completed the stadium in Colon that ranks second to none. You are a very popular young man in Panama, so I think it is fitting that the Colon team has asked me to request that you pitch the first three innings of their opening night game next week."

At home the kid was taught never to judge anyone by the color of their skin. Thus, Apartheid was repugnant to him. So he answered affirmatively with but one proviso: would anyone object if he used his first and middle name because of the severe heat he will have to take if the Base found out? The man smiled. "I understand," he said.

The newspaper and radio hype about the opening game all listed the starting line-ups with all Spanish surnames, except one, "The Kid's." Game time came and the umpires announced the batteries for the night. The kid stepped up out of the dugout. A cheer went up all over the stadium. About half the attendees wore the U.S. military uniform. He performed his stint successfully, took a shower and arrived back in the barracks by 11:00 PM, and promptly went to bed.

He was awakened by the First Sergeant just after dawn next morning, and told to report immediately to the orderly room.  Hurriedly, he dressed and descended the stairs as ordered.  Deep down inside, he knew the "cat was out of the bag."  Around a conference table sat, among others, the oldest in-grade First Lieutenant, who had a deep-rooted dislike of all enlisted types especially northerners.

The kid never forgot that man.  He personified all the rot connected with  Army Caste system practiced in that day and age.  He also represented the Apartheid system in the Panama Canal Zone in the "thirties" which the kid had crossed at such a great personal risk.

The caste system can best be illustrated by an incident involving the great entertainer, Al Jolson. A couple of days before Jolson was due to perform with a USO troupe, the kid and several other "doggies" were ordered to prepare one of the hangars on the flight line for the great event.  They labored long and hard to clean up the place while a crew from the construction unit built a stage in the center of the hangar.  They set up a hundred or more folding chairs delivered by the Quartermaster squadron.

When the great moment arrived, Mr. Jolson walked out on the stage and looked about.  Inside the hangar seated in the rows of folding chairs were officers and their ladies.  He walked off the stage in disgust.  He sent for the Base Commander.  Jolson said:  "I came here to entertain the troops.  I see nothing but officers inside this place.  The troops are standing outside in the hot sun where they can neither hear nor see the program very well.  The officers can afford to pay for their entertainment, the troops cannot.  I demand that all the officers and their ladies leave and that the troops be brought inside. Otherwise, Colonel, there will be no show."  In a matter of minutes the officer crowd angrily removed themselves and the show went on with all the doggies seated in the folding chairs.

Apparently, the newspapers had a field day about the kid's participation in the Panamanian baseball event, pointing out that the kid was the first white in the country's history to ever cross the color line in sports competition.  Big banner headlines leaped out at him from the desk.  And he felt a surge of pride right down to the bottom of his feet.

Although a Major was the Squadron Commander the First Lieutenant appeared to be in charge of the meeting. The Major sat quietly in the rear.  The Lieutenant  was livid and appeared to be emotionally out of control.  He fairly screamed at the kid:  "You have created an international incident in which the Governor General of the Canal Zone has been embarrassed. You are getting far too much publicity for an enlisted man. Furthermore, orders have been cut for your immediate transfer to the gunnery range out in the interior of Panama. Report to the flight-line immediately for transportation by aircraft to Rio Hato."

The kid arrived at the interior post and was assigned to a barracks. At Rio Hato he performed such duties as searching the grounds, in early morning, for worms, bugs, etc. to feed the Commander's monkeys or for some other such nonsense. The Commander's monkeys used for the purpose of searching the mattresses of enlisteds for bedbugs. Such inspections were to determine if enlisteds had obeyed regulations that called for the weekly spraying of mattresses.

At the Rio Hato base, the kid had the dubious honor of driving the base Commander's old Ford roadster around the base with an outhouse perched on the rumble seat. He performed all other kinds of humiliating, degrading duties, which according to Army regulations, were not to be performed by noncommissioned officers. The kid had no access to the Inspector General's office, however, he did hear that an investigation followed his exit from there. The Commander was relieved of his post and subsequently given a medical discharge.

About six weeks had elapsed, until one morning, when the kid went out to duty, he was confronted with a wild-eyed Major from France Field. The Major ordered him to get his gear out of the barracks. He said: "I'm here to take you back to France Field. Whoever in hell ordered you up here is in deep trouble. The Colonel is mad as hell!"

Arriving back at France Field was like entering a tomb. The silent treatment was in place. No one would talk to him. So the kid decided it was time to do what he should have done when he arrived at the Base. He told the team manager, "I'm not playing baseball any more unless I work on airplanes." Shock waves ran the gamut and the kid was summoned to the Squadron's First Sergeant's office.

General Patton's personality had just become popular to some on the base. His appearance, at the Louisiana maneuvers, with the pearl handled pistols, strapped to his hips, had received great media play.

The kid arrived at the Orderly Room and there stood the "Top Kick" all dressed up with two-gun holsters on his big fat hips displaying pearl handled pistols. With great difficulty, the kid choked back laughter. The First Sergeant said: "I understand you are having a temperamental fit about playing baseball. Well, if you don't want to play baseball, I can't make you play. But I can sure as hell make you wish you were playing. For starters, you report to the Sergeant across the road over there in the jungle and start hacking brush with a machete."

Across the road, the kid discovered a crew of guys from the stockade, and other malefactors, who had been chopping jungle brush, were admiring the size of a big Bushmaster snake. That serpent sent chills up and down the kid's spine but he vowed to himself that he would stick it out inasmuch as one of the prisoners made some snide remark about how far the big baseball hero had fallen.

He was out there long enough to work up a big sweat when a staff car pulled up along side the road. The Flight Surgeon, Captain Morely, stepped out and called to him. The Captain said: "Get into the car, you're going to the infirmary with me."

When they arrived at the infirmary, he assigned the kid to a room: "Go in there, take off your clothes and get into bed! The idea of treating one of the best assets this base has ever had in this manner is ridiculous. If the Colonel was here, some heads would roll. Why, do you know that during the baseball season the venereal disease rate on the Base dropped to almost nil?" said the Captain.

The kid had been in the Captain's care about an hour when he heard a ruckus out in the office. The First Lieutenant and his "gunny" were after his hide. The flight surgeon laid down the law of his office: "For your information, Lieutenant, your authority does not extend to my medical facility nor does it supersede my medical judgment as a doctor. Now be off with you!"

The kid was there for two days, and then released as cured of whatever it was they said he had. The Colonel was back. After a short conference in his office, the kid was transferred out of the squadron and assigned to the flight line in another squadron. The Colonel had two requests: "Will you resume your play in the winter league? I enjoy going down there Sundays to watch you toy with the big guys. "Incidentally," he said: "I'd like to be your manager. I'm getting all kinds of inquiries from the Yankees, Red Sox, Cardinals, and the Saint Louis Browns about your future when you get out of the service next Fall. I want to make sure you to get the best deal," he added.

The kid got the best deal offered for the next Fall. It was offered by the Yankees who wanted him to report to their Kansas City farm club in Haines City, Florida in February 1942. By then World War II was underway and the kid eventually wound up as crew Chief of a P-38 with the First Fighter Group in Italy.

While exiled in Rio Hato, the kid traveled back to France Field one weekend to take a Flight Engineer's exam. At the time, he scored in the top ten among the participants on the Base. In order to return to Rio Hato, he went to the flightline to hitch a ride. He was successful.

A Douglas A-20A was leaving for the same destination. The vow he had made back home, as a little kid, never to use a parachute under any circumstance was nearly broken that Sunday afternoon in 1939, high above Chorroro Flats, along the Pacific coast of Panama.

The Army Air Corps Douglas A-20A airplane, in which he was flying, began to fall apart when the pilot attempted to perform a maneuver for which the airplane was not designed. The A-20A was powered by two 1600 hp Wright R2699-11 engines. Equipped with two- speed superchargers, the A-20A had a top speed of 325 mph in level flight.

The weather was perfect with a gentle breeze blowing across their nose. Rio Hato was not far off. Suddenly they were interdicted by a formation of Curtiss P-36 fighter aircraft out of Albrooke Field who wanted to play. Using below tree top evasive tactics, by flying up the Canyons in the area, the A-20A pilot managed to escape the fighters. The friendly game of hide and seek continued on for quite some time. But, all at once, as suddenly as they had appeared, the fighters were gone.

Perhaps spurred on by a sudden rush of adrenaline, built up during the chase, the pilot blasted the engines to full throttle. From the floor of a canyon, the big airplane hung on the props until it reached an altitude of slightly over 15,000 feet. At that level, he rolled the big ship over, and then, from an inverted attitude, he again blasted the engines wide open into a horrendous power dive.

The high-pitched scream of the engines hit the kid's ears like daggers scraping across his ear drums. Blue flame (St. Elmo's fire) danced, shimmering across the wings and, as he watched, from his uncomfortable perch, looking out at the rear from the rear gunner's seat, he saw large chunks of the tail section floating away from the airplane.

He glanced out over the wings. It appeared as though some great giant had hit each wing root, with the heel of his hand, rippling the metal skin all the way out to the tips. For some strange reason this model airplane, which was basically metal, featured fabric covered ailerons, and tail section. He struggled to get his arms up to reach the escape hatch handle but found it to be useless. He could not move. "G" forces nailed his body to the back of the seat. He prayed.

Slowly, the big airplane began to move out of the vertical dive and up into a recovery close to a normal flight attitude. It was at that point, that the pilot's efforts to recover began to take effect. The airplane leveled out momentarily and then began to climb. The pilot wrestled with the controls and finally returned the crippled ship to near normal flight again.

By that time, stark reality had penetrated the pilot's thick skull. He asked for an assessment of the damage to the airplane. The kid gave him the message about the tail section and aileron damage. After a short pause, he arrived at the conclusion that the airplane was increasingly difficult to control and quite possibly could get worse. At best they were in deep trouble.

After some discussion with the guy in front, a Major, the pilot then gave the bailout command. When the kid attempted to "pop" the escape hatch, he discovered that the latch handle, securing the hatch over the gunner's cockpit, had been wired shut from the outside, no doubt by some "BB" brain, to keep it from rattling. A gun platform, located on the floor of the cockpit, opened downward to freedom, or so he thought. He had found new hope. But hope was short-lived. When he attempted to turn the hand crank that operated the platform, he discovered it was jammed shut by twisted, warped fuselage metal. It could not be moved.

The kid hurriedly communicated his dilemma to the pilot who immediately turned off the intercom. He wondered if the pilot and the Major would determine that the airplane could not make it to Albrooke Field and thus, bail out; better to sacrifice one life than lose all three.

The kid was already blubbering out a prayer; saying to God: "I'm too young to die. I have so much to live for; so many things to do." However, the pilot, after conferring with the Major, said: "Hang on Sarge. We are going back to

Albrooke Field. Hold on for the hottest landing you'll ever witness."

With most of the rudder gone and severe damage to the airframe and wings, the pilot managed to steer a course to the southeast by partially maneuvering the airplane with the throttles. On the approach to Albrooke, they dropped down over a big hump of solid rock, on the glide path, near the end of the runway.

The big ship flared out over railroad tracks, a field of stumps, and then down onto the end of the runway. They were traveling at a tremendous rate of speed that had been built up by maneuvering the airplane with the throttles.

The speed was too great to overcome so there was little or no chance for the pilot to hold the airplane off the runway, a method ordinarily used to reduce landing speed. Even under normal circumstances the airplane had a glide angle of a 40-ton rock rolling off a cliff.

The huge, heavy airplane hit the runway at approximately a 45 degree angle. The landing speed must have been more than a hundred miles per hour. From his position, sitting backward in the rear cockpit, the kid watched as the tires peeled off the wheels and hurtled out of sight across the field.

The airplane continued on, sliding sideways. Strangely, the kid heard no sound. Sparks showered out from behind the landing gear wheels like the trailing of gigantic sky rockets, and for the first time, he thought about fire.

Fire trucks, crash trucks and ambulances chased them down the runway. The airplane finally stopped sliding and came to an abrupt stop. The fuselage rolled up and over into an inverted position, as though in a slow motion film.

It seemed like they were still moving when rescue crews were cutting open the gun platform which was now up over the bottom of his feet, as he hung upside down on the safety harness. He heard someone yell to alert firemen about a small fire that had started on one of the engines. He heard the blast of the fire extinguisher and relaxed. Loud voices were instructing him not to release the safety harness.

After what seemed to be an eternity, they lifted the bottom platform away, slid a lifting-sling under his body, released the safety harness, turned his body right side up, and pulled him up out of the cockpit. When he reached the top, the crews were lined up waiting for him. He dropped down to the cement on the opposite side of the wreckage.

After all, he had to show them that he was not afraid lest they think otherwise.

To regain his composure, he slowly, and somewhat wobbly, walked around the wreckage. The Major in the Bombardier's seat, up front in the nose, appeared to be badly injured. The kid heard something concerning a severe head injury and they were concerned that his neck or back may have been broken.

As for the kid's condition: after the rescue guys lifted him out of the cockpit, he was able to walk to the ambulance for the mandatory ride to the medical facility. No injuries of a substantial nature were found. He was able to hitchhike to his destination where he arrived just before midnight thanks to an ancient Panamanian and his ancient truck. He spoke no English so the kid had a chance to spend some quiet time during which he thanked the Lord profusely for sparing his life.

Later that night he awoke in a cold sweat, shaking like a leaf in a hurricane. He was awake throughout the night caught in the, "what if," anxiety mode. By the morning's light, he was back to his usual cool, calm, stoic self.

As the result of the incident and the pilot's erroneous report, all A-20As in the Air Corps were immediately grounded until the cause could be determined. It took no time at all for an investigation to get underway and for the accident investigators to determine the cause.

The Accident Review Board, after an extremely short deliberation, decided that the pilot's poor judgment and clumsy attempts to cover it up made him "professionally unqualified for flying." The pilot did not react kindly to the Board's decision. Moreover, he blamed not himself for his behavior, but the Major and the kid for "squealing" on him, as he called their version of what happened.

So much for Army flying and the mass training and assignments to aircraft that many novice pilots were not psychologically equipped to fly, or were just plain incompetent. The kid dealt with flight instructors that he would rather face a court-martial than fly with.

There were several characters that made the Island Crop Dusting Company such an interesting and exciting place for a youngster like the kid to get a start in the world of aviation. They gave him a start that lasted 55 years. All the guys who made up the Island Crop Dusting Company, at one time or another, were good to him. They were all in their mid-twenties to early thirties. He learned something of value from every one of them. Oddly enough, no one ever treated him like the dumb kid he really was.

The kid would never have made it in life had it not been for Ernie Pretsch and the guys that made up the Island Crop Dusting Company. In the main, Ernie, and The Island Crop Dusting Company crew gave him the desire and the tools and the courage needed to make something of himself. The kid suspected, right from the beginning, that they both were doomed to something much better, but a whole lot duller.

Neither Ernie nor anyone else, not even a Hollywood casting director, could have assembled a better cast of characters; each one was a gem in his own way. The kid learned something of value from each one of them, especially from Ernie.

Moreover, from the time Ernie said, "Hi kid!" he had felt a great load of self doubt come off his being; a load that had been as heavy as the weight of the world. And once he had achieved something, such as flying an airplane all by himself, his self confidence took off.

What he learned from The Island Crop Dusting Company became the tools he used, after the war, to get a college degree, and live a happy, successful life, with a 45 year career in aviation and aerospace. And now, most of all, he is left with a lot of great memories, memories of what was really accomplished by his whole experience with the Island Crop Dusting Company.

THE JENNY WAS FIRST WITH BARNSTORMERS LIKE GEORGE SHAW AND CHARLES LINDBERGH. THEY INSPIRED THEIR DESCENDANTS INCLUDING YOUNG ERNIE PRETSCH TO SPREAD THE FLYING BUG ALL OVER AMERICA.